Tales Jesus Told

Tales Jesus Told

An Introduction to the Narrative Parables of Jesus

Stephen I. Wright

PATERNOSTER PRESS

Copyright © 2002 Stephen I. Wright

First published in 2002 by Paternoster Press

08 07 06 05 04 03 02   7 6 5 4 3 2 1

Paternoster Press is an imprint of Authentic Media,
P.O. Box 300, Carlisle, Cumbria, CA3 0QS, UK
and
P.O. Box 1047, Waynesboro, GA 30830-2047, USA

www.paternoster-publishing.com

The right of Stephen I. Wright to be identified as the Author of this Work
has been asserted by him in accordance with the Copyright,
Designs and Patents Act 1988.

British Library Cataloguing in Publication Data
A catalogue record for this book is available from the British Library

ISBN 1-84227-182-2

Unless otherwise stated, Scripture quotations are taken from the
NEW REVISED STANDARD VERSION BIBLE,
copyright 1989,
Division of Christian Education of the National Council
of the Churches of Christ in the United States of America.
Used by permission. All rights reserved.

Cover Design by FourNineZero
Typeset by WestKey Ltd, Falmouth, Cornwall
Printed in Great Britain by Cox & Wyman Ltd, Reading, Berkshire

For Linda

The order of perception in a parable is such that it keeps our eyes on our world and that world as transformed by God, not on 'God in himself'.

Sallie McFague

Contents

Foreword

You may have been in conversation with someone who's told a story or joke and you've just not got it! They laugh uproariously and you feign a smile, hoping the penny might drop – and it doesn't. You might or might not say 'Sorry, I didn't get it.' You've failed to get the point because you've not understood the nuances and the niceties of the story or the language.

The parables of Jesus present the same sort of difficulty. Familiar though they are to many Christians we fail to grasp their true meaning because we don't fully understand the culture in which Jesus lived and told his stories. We miss the point and often the joke.

Stephen Wright takes us on a guided tour of the world of the parables of Jesus. Like an interpreter explaining language and customs to a band of foreign tourists he opens up the true meaning of the stories of Jesus.

It's important to know that Jesus told stories primarily to adults and not to children, although I should imagine that most of his audiences comprised people of all ages.

These stories are often humorous, sometimes poignant, always challenging and full of surprises. In these pages Stephen throws light on the parables of Jesus so that there will be times in this book when you'll say, 'Oh, that's what it's all about!' Stephen brings to this delightful task the weight of his academic knowledge but with a lightness of touch that will keep you reading on.

In 1 Corinthians 13 Saint Paul says that for now we see through a glass darkly. In the original script Paul does not use the word 'darkly'. Instead he uses a phrase 'in an enigma'. On this shore we do not have the language of heaven to explain divine mysteries. All we have are enigmas, similes, metaphors, allegories and parables. This was the language that Jesus used to speak of God's presence in this crazy yet beautiful world and to tell of God's kingdom. In this book Stephen exercises the gift of interpretation. The proof of this rests with the reader!

The Rt Revd James Jones
August 2002

Introduction

In this book I attempt an introduction to the longer narrative parables of Jesus. Books on the parables are numerous, but I have felt for several years that certain well-established trends in parable interpretation have been somewhat misguided. Not the least of these trends has been the tendency to disparage the interpretations of the early church as 'spiritualizing' while continuing to offer spiritualizing readings in various twentieth-century guises. I suggest that in the twenty-first Christian century it is time to take a more intense look at these stories against their original social background.

I hope the book will speak for itself, and I have tried to let it do so in a way that will be accessible to anyone with an interest in literature or the ancient world, Christian or not, scholar or not. I want to suggest the interest and attractiveness of the stories, and that purpose is dangerously compromised by a full scholarly apparatus of footnotes! There is a place for a full scholarly treatment, and perhaps one day I will be able to offer it. There is also a place for a fresh treatment of the story of the parables' interpretation over the years, and for an exploration of the profound ways in which they engage with contemporary concerns, and may be dramatized and retold so as to capture imaginations afresh. But these things are for another time. For now, I have felt sufficiently convinced of the coherence and importance of the approach that I am advocating to want to lay it out in as straightforward a manner as I can, concentrating on what appears to have been the thrust of the tales in their original setting.

The main detailed research and theoretical thinking that lies beneath this book is set out in my *The Voice of Jesus: Studies in the Interpretation of Six Gospel Parables*. I also draw on work that I did on three of the parables for a symposium at McMaster Divinity College, Hamilton, Ontario in June 1998, which appeared as 'Parables on Poverty and Riches' in the book that resulted from the gathering, *The Challenge of Jesus' Parables*. I am grateful to the convenor of the symposium and editor of the book, Dr Richard Longenecker, for his invitation to participate, and to other participants for the stimulus of that event and for their contributions.

Since I am not indicating in the text the detail of my dependence on others it is right that I express at this point my deep indebtedness to scholars much more learned than myself. I must name three. The first two I have never met. Kenneth E. Bailey's studies of the Luke parables, *Poet and Peasant* and *Through Peasant Eyes*, have been a rich source of information and inspiration from one steeped in the culture of the Middle East. William R. Herzog II's *Parables as Subversive Speech: Jesus as Pedagogue of the Oppressed* applies sociological studies of the ancient world to the parables with a thoroughness and directness – not to mention a touch of iconoclasm! – that I have found very refreshing. My differences, in certain ways, from both these scholars should be taken as a compliment to their profound influence on my thinking. The third scholar I must name is my brother, Tom Wright. His works on Jesus and the first century have been seminal in my consideration of the background of the parables. Those who are familiar with them will recognize both the extent of his influence and the points of difference. It is a privilege to have such a discussion partner in the family.

All these works, and others that may be found useful by readers wishing to delve deeper into the subject, are listed in a bibliography at the end of this book. Having written the book, I feel more than ever that it is indeed but an introduction to the stories. It offers an interpretation, but there is so much gold to be found by those who will pick up the clues and search further and deeper – a search that may sometimes lead to quite new and different insights.

I am grateful to my colleague Pieter Lalleman for reading and commenting on several draft chapters.

I wrote this book at home in the evenings when the rest of the day's work was done. I am therefore especially grateful to my family for their patience. Many have been the evenings when my sons Tristan and Laurence have had to forgo chatting on the Internet because I was hogging the computer. My daughter Tamsin has urged me repeatedly to write something that was not 'complicated blah-blah' (for a change, that is!). I fear that I may need still to explain a few words to her, but I have tried! My wife Linda has persistently and faithfully encouraged me with the belief that the book was needed and that I could write it, and has helped me to persevere. I dedicate it to her with much love.

1

The Parables of Jesus

About Jesus of Nazareth there is one striking fact, among others, on which historians agree: he told stories. We have a written record of some of them in the books we know as the Gospels of Matthew, Mark and Luke, in the collection we know as the New Testament. A few also appear in the so-called 'Gospel of Thomas', a collection of sayings purporting to go back to Jesus. The name generally given to these stories is *parables*.

Some of the stories have become world famous. That of the Good Samaritan, for example, has given its hero's description to the English language. Others are much less well known. But the familiar ones too have strange, sometimes disturbing aspects, which easily get forgotten, even in the communities of Jesus' followers that continue to preserve his memory.

This book sets out to introduce the parables of Jesus to those who feel either unfamiliar or overfamiliar with them. There have been numerous scholarly works devoted to this subject, and I am indebted to many of them. But I do not wish to enter into many fine details of scholarly argument here. I hope, rather, simply to suggest something of the purpose and effect of Jesus' stories by reading them against the background of his situation in first-century Palestine.

Why read the parables?

The parables are of interest on many counts. They are among the most memorable passages in the Bible. They are unique in style in ancient literature – a fact that can be obscured by their familiarity within the church. They represent a characteristically Jewish mode of teaching, but remain rather different from the large number of parables that have survived from the Jewish rabbis of Jesus' time and after. They have inspired many works of art and countless sermons. They have significantly shaped Christian under-standings of God – even though the great fourth-century teacher Jerome advised (wisely) against building doctrine on the foundation of a parable. But perhaps the deepest reason for interest in the parables is that, by general agree-ment, they take us as near to the mind and mission of Jesus as any other text we have.

Here a word of caution is necessary. The parables have a distinct whiff of individuality about them, which convinces most readers that they are indeed authentic stories of Jesus. But this does not mean that we can say with confidence about any one of them that we know what Jesus *meant* by it. Such statements about Jesus' 'meaning' not only often go beyond a sober reckoning of how far we can enter into the mind of an ancient figure through reading a record of their words – particularly the words of a story that may not *directly* reveal much about the teller. Statements of a parable's 'meaning' also usually end up diminishing the power of the story by being too dogmatic. Stories in any case do not lend themselves to being reduced to an 'explanation'. Even though stories like these are short and sharp, there will always be more to them than any state-ment of their 'meaning' can convey. We ought anyway to think as much in terms of 'effect' as of 'meaning'; of what the parables were designed to *do* as much as what they were intended to *say*. They linger in the mind, provoking us to go on thinking, and revising the way we see the world.

Having issued this caution, however, there is no reason why the parables should not be taken as yielding insight into the thinking and purpose of Jesus. A fresh look at the parables may especially be useful in countering misleading impressions about him that can easily arise twenty centuries on, among his followers as well as others. There is indeed a particular angle on life, an interpretation and questioning of accepted realities, which can be discerned in these stories and which retains the power to haunt us today.

Hence this book is an *introduction* to the parables rather than an attempt at a full *explanation* of them. I aim to give enough background information to suggest the kind of thrust the stories would probably have had for their first hearers, but then to do as Jesus did: be quiet and let them do their own work. In this way we may be able to get a clearer glimpse of Jesus' outlook and intentions without deceiving ourselves that we can see more than is really possible. But we will also be able to open ourselves to the mysterious force of these ancient tales with that self-surrender that is the prerequisite for receiving and appreciating all created art, not least the spoken narrative.

What is a parable?

Various definitions of a 'parable' have been given. Words in the Bible that are sometimes translated into English as 'parable' have a range of meanings in the original Hebrew and Greek. The stories Jesus told, which we usually call 'parables', are often not given that name in the text. But it is helpful to try to put our finger on the kind of stories they are, while always being open to the possibility that as we listen to them more, they will force us to revise our definition.

A popular old definition was 'earthly story with heavenly meaning', but this can be misleading. It implies that to get the real point of a parable we have to look right *away* from the happenings in the everyday world that it relates, to some 'spiritual' or invisible reality. It is better to see a parable as inviting us to look *at* the everyday world with new eyes. This fits too with the Hebrew word *mashal*, which lies behind the usage of the word 'parable' in the New Testament, and can be used of a whole range of 'wise sayings', proverbs and riddles.

Sometimes the word 'parable' is applied to sayings that are not stories but vivid word-pictures. By all accounts, the language Jesus used was highly pictorial. It does not matter where we draw the line as to what is and is not technically a 'parable'. The important thing is to let our minds and imaginations be open to this powerful, suggestive language, whether it comes in story form or not. In this book we shall look only at 'parables' that are stories in the strict sense of the word. There is something unique about the shape of a story, the invitation it implies to its hearers: 'think about this', 'imagine this'.

Mostly, the written records we have of Jesus' parables do not include any extended explanation or interpretation. We shall discuss the two notable exceptions to this, the stories of the sower and of the wheat and the darnel, when we come to them. Often there are just a few words of application to the hearers. Sometimes the story itself is left completely alone to do its job, though the context in which it comes in the Gospel where it is found usually gives a hint as to why Jesus told it.

Scholars have often thought that the explanations and applications of the parables that are found in the Gospels are the work of Jesus' followers, who handed the stories on, rather than being original to Jesus himself. But it is difficult and unwise at this distance in time to think that we can neatly separate off words of interpretation from the parables themselves. It would be quite natural if the Gospel writers (and those who handed the stories on to them) shaped the parables with an eye to the needs of their own hearers and readers. Like preachers in every generation, they will have framed the stories in a way suitable to their audience. At the same time, it would have been quite natural for Jesus to have added words of explanation to his stories from time to time.

In this book I shall not go into much detail discussing which parts of the parable records are original to Jesus and which parts are the interpretations of his followers. This can turn into a rather arid exercise whose results are always bound to be uncertain and debatable. Rather, I shall concentrate on what the parable as a realistic story may have suggested to Jesus' audiences, and how it may have provoked them. I am therefore working with the general assumption that, where we see odd turns of phrase that seem out of place in a realistic story, they come from the early Christians' reflections on the story's significance in the light of what they had come to believe about Jesus. In the penultimate chapter we will glance at this rich tradition of parable interpretation, starting from very soon after the time of Jesus himself.

First, however, let us fill in some of the background, which can help us to feel the impact of these tales and to imagine intelligently the purpose of the one who first told them.

2

Jesus and First-Century Palestine

Palestine in the first century

The Jewish people had lived under the rule of the Romans since 63 BC and under Greek domination for many years previous to that. Although Roman rule could be harsh and at times brutal it suited the overlords to allow a certain degree of liberty to their subject peoples. So, provided it did not directly threaten Roman supremacy, the Jews could practise their ancestral faith. Indeed, in the time of Jesus, a magnificent new Temple was under construction on the site of its predecessors in Jerusalem. This was the scene of animal sacrifices and the focus for worship of the one the Jewish people revered as 'the Lord', the God who had shown himself to their forebear Abraham some two thousand years previously, and who, they believed, had been the guiding hand behind their history ever since.

The complex political machinations that occur when a small nation is living in an uneasy truce with a greater ruling power can readily be imagined. It is precisely such a complex situation into which our sources for the history of the period, notably the four Gospels and the writings of the Jewish historian Josephus, give us a glimpse. The part-Jewish Herod family were puppet rulers up until the brutal suppression of the Jewish revolt against Rome in 66–70 CE, when Jerusalem was razed to the ground.

Various groups within Judaism can be roughly seen as representing different attitudes towards the Roman authorities. The Sadducees were members of the wealthy ruling priestly class of Jews, in control of the Temple. They owed their continuing position to the Romans and were thus anxious not to upset them. The Pharisees were a kind of pressure group, concerned that the Jews should maintain their ancestral traditions, despite the heavy hand of Rome. They saw the strict observance of the law as the key to maintaining the identity of the Jews as 'Israel', God's people. They drew on oral traditions to apply the written law to every situation of life. Especially, they wanted to see the purity system, which technically applied only to the priests and Temple staff, extended to apply to everyone. 'Zealots' is the name loosely applied to a variety of groups of different degrees of lawlessness and violence who believed in the violent overthrow of their oppressors as the way forward for Israel. The Essenes were a group who withdrew from mainstream Jewish life entirely, believing the Temple and its priests to be corrupt. They had their own 'alternative' sacrificial system and looked to God to overthrow not only the Romans but also the 'apostate' Jewish leadership. A rich if sometimes puzzling record of their isolated desert communities is found in the Dead Sea Scrolls.

These, however, were particular prominent groups who, even combined, made up only a small minority of the Jewish population. What of the majority? This was an agrarian society made up largely of peasant farmers and their families. They lived close to the breadline, working small plots of land that had been handed down through many generations. For many, however, the burdens of taxation imposed not only by the Romans but also by the Temple authorities made survival a constant struggle.

Many ended up virtual or actual slaves to wealthy land-owners. Some slaves found themselves in positions of considerable trust and responsibility, though of course at the cost of their independence.

When families grew too large for the land to support them, some individuals might have to take their chance in the insecure market for day labouring, or, worse still, sink into a life of begging. Some people, of course, had positions that brought them in more cash income than a peasant farmer could hope to get: estate managers, tax and toll collectors, merchants, soldiers and others. But life for these people was not necessarily much more secure than that of the peasants, not least because their work entailed a lot of contact with their wealthy (usually Roman) employers. They were therefore under the suspicion of many of their fellow Jews, who could see the sharp practice that such work often involved, and who regarded entanglement with the Gentile oppressors as undermining Jewish distinctiveness.

Jesus himself was born into a family that belonged to yet another social grouping. Learning his trade as a carpenter, he grew up as one of the artisan class. They would probably have been a little better off than the average peasant family. However, there was no 'middle class' in our modern sense. The great overriding social division that dominated the whole of life was that between a tiny number of (for those days) very rich landowners and the great majority of the population who could fairly be described as – more or less – poor.

What about the faith of the Jewish people? This played a profound and formative role in the whole of their existence. There were many variations in belief and practice, but some strong common attitudes and expectations. They believed that the creator of the world had called them to be a special people who knew his purposes and his ways and were thus able to reveal him to the world. They believed that their land was God's gift to them and therefore sacred. They believed that Jerusalem was a holy city and the Temple the focus of God's presence. And they believed that somehow, sooner or later, he would rescue them from oppression and liberate them to live out their calling in peace. A number probably used the term 'the kingdom of God' for this hoped-for state.

Jesus of Nazareth

Very soon after his death at the hands of the Roman authorities in about 30 CE Jesus of Nazareth became the focal figure of a new movement within Judaism. He was worshipped as 'Lord' (hitherto a name for God alone) and 'Christ' ('Messiah', that is, 'Anointed One') by followers who were convinced that God had raised him from death. These adherents, who some years later were to become known as 'Christians', were drawn from a nucleus of those who had followed him before his death and a widening circle of both Jews and Gentiles across the Roman Empire. Their allegiance to Jesus inevitably led to tensions with others within Judaism, especially because they proclaimed his resurrection. The significance of this assertion was its implication that God had vindicated one whom some of his own compatriots had conspired to do away with. Not surprisingly, the groups of 'Christians' gradually became separate from the rest of Judaism, a separation that was effectively complete by the end of the first century CE. The church was born.

So familiar has the name of Jesus become to many over the centuries, in and through the church that continues to worship him, that sometimes the significance of what he said and did in the few years of his public activity *before* he was crucified has been overlooked, especially by devout

Christians. The parables, of course, belong to this period. On the other hand, over the last couple of centuries there have been periods of intense historical investigation into the nature of Jesus' intentions, the circumstances of his life and the causes of his death. The debate continues to be lively and many points are disputed. The evidence of the four Gospels is partial, and scholars argue over which parts may in fact say more about the faith of the early Christians than the life of Jesus, which is their ostensible subject. What, though, can be reasonably said about Jesus that will help us better to understand the stories he told?

He was a wandering teacher or prophet

Jesus acquired the reputation of a wandering rabbi (teacher), though we do not read anything in the Gospels about any official authorization as such. He went from one town or village to another, teaching not only in their synagogues (meeting houses for worship), but in the open air. His activity and his teaching bore many of the hallmarks of the prophets, individuals who had spoken on God's behalf to the Israelite people and rulers between roughly the ninth and the fifth centuries BC. They had explained current events in the light of God's purpose, summoned people to return to obedience to God's law, and pronounced judgement upon nations – including Israel itself – but had also held out a beacon of hope for Israel and for the world. They had used vivid, powerful language to get their message across. The word-pictures drawn by Jesus in his parables are in some ways similar to those that had been used by the prophets. He too did not speak of God in abstract fashion but let a God-inspired faith shed a searchlight on the world.

The voice of prophecy was generally reckoned by the Jewish people to have been silent for about four hundred years by the time of Jesus. However, he had one immediate precursor, his older contemporary and cousin John the Baptist. John was a lone but forceful preacher who had begun a movement of national repentance and who met his death after confronting the ruler, Herod, about his immoral relationships.

The element of Jesus' teaching that most connects him with the prophets was the authority with which he spoke. Unlike the normal style of rabbinic teaching, which revolved around explaining and applying the ancient law believed to have been given to the people through Moses, Jesus' approach seemed fresh. Although we have records of him discussing matters of law with the experts, most of his recorded teaching does not consist of explications of the law, but of words apparently spoken on his own authority. His parables are a prime example of such words. But they are also, in their indirect, understated style, interestingly different from the fiery denunciations and exuberant promises that fill many of the pages of Old Testament prophecy.

He spoke about the kingdom of God

A common theme of Jesus' teaching, indeed the unifying theme according to many scholars, was 'the kingdom of God'. It was a fundamental Jewish belief that their God was king over all the earth. But how was this kingship visible? It certainly would not have seemed to many that God was king when his own people were under the thumb of Roman oppression. Many Jews, it seems, expected God to come and reveal his kingship once and for all with a decisive display of power, overthrowing his enemies. Jesus said that the kingdom of God was indeed 'at hand': God would defeat his enemies. However, in all sorts of ways he warned that it would not come in the way that many expected. Above all, the nearness of God's kingdom meant that his people should repent. Having Jewish ancestry was no guarantee that one would enjoy the benefits of God's rule. If God was going to show he was king, this did not mean that his children should take up arms and fight their enemies – it meant that they had to return to a profound obedience to him.

A number of the parables are explicitly linked to the kingdom of God in the Gospel records. It seems likely that Jesus did sometimes make it clear when telling a story that he was saying something about God's kingdom. It is equally likely that on many occasions he drew no such specific link. But the pictures in many parables of a world that runs on different lines from that which people commonly experienced make it a natural conclusion that he was communicating his vision of God's kingdom.

He called people to follow him

Jesus did not 'teach' in an abstract fashion. He gathered a following who became intensely committed to him as a person, even though they seem to have found many of his sayings hard to understand, and, no doubt, still harder to put into practice. For Jesus, it was of paramount importance that the mission to which he felt himself called was a shared mission. Others were to be involved in its joys and its burdens. His setting aside of an inner group of twelve disciples (those who became known as the 'apostles') seems designed to have echoes of the ancient makeup of Israel as twelve tribes. It was as if Jesus was indicating that the time had come for a completely new start for Israel, beginning with these twelve men gathered around himself.

There were times, though, when Jesus needed to warn people who seemed over-eager to follow him. Such people may have thought that being in his company would put them on the right side in an imminent God-backed uprising against the Romans. Some may have simply been jumping on the latest bandwagon. Jesus said, correctly, that following him all the way would lead to suffering and death. He knew that the path he had charted was bound to bring him into conflict with the Jewish authorities, and that nothing he said about God being king would endear him to the Romans, either.

The parables give glimpses and hints, through the portrayal of a character or scene, of something of the cost entailed in going Jesus' way. But they also communicate a sense of the joy of doing so. And some, more darkly, paint a picture of the misery that rejecting the commands of God must bring.

He healed sick people and spent time with the outcast

Jesus' mission involved him in far more than words. He was a healer through whom people recognized God's power at work. But this healing activity was something quite different from mere wonder working or magic tricks. It was seen, especially in retrospect, as the fulfilment of old prophetic promises of a time when God would renew his creation. It was much more, too, than the restoration of bodily health. Most of the records of Jesus' healing involve individuals whose condition cut them off from the life of society. Skin diseases, haemorrhages, disordered personalities, even those states we now think of simply as 'disability', such as blindness and deafness, all kept those who suffered them at arm's length from family and community. It was to preserve the community's own sense of wholeness that such people were kept on the margins. Through healing them Jesus also restored them to participation in the community's life.

Nor was it only the physically troubled to whom Jesus became the outstretched arm of human friendship. The Gospels report his association with those on the edges of

society for other reasons – those engaged in pursuits considered dubious and tainting by the majority, such as collecting
customs for the Romans, or even prostitution. Jesus risked,
and earned, the disapproval of many for this association.
It seems that for him restoration of Israel's health as a
community could only be accomplished if he took the lead
in befriending those whom the mainstream rejected.

This aspect of Jesus' activity is clearly reflected in his
parables too. A number of them portray the outcast being
welcomed, the rejected forgiven, the unclean accepted.
In this sense the stories reflect the kind of events that,
following Jesus' lead, were actually coming about.

Why did Jesus tell stories?

How, then, do the parables fit with the rest of Jesus' activity?
May we detect any unifying theme within them or purpose
behind them? What was the significance of the fact that
he told so many *stories*? We will be in a better position to
answer this question once we have looked at the stories in
detail. But let us make a few preliminary comments.

We notice first of all that, according to the Gospels, Jesus
told stories in many different contexts. Looking at these
contexts we may gain an impression of the versatility of
both the story form and the storyteller. We may also guard
against too 'heavy' an approach to understanding them.
Jesus seems to have had a lightness of touch. One can imagine him chuckling at some of the earnest, po-faced attempts
to analyse and interpret his stories.

So, for example, we find Jesus using stories with a crowd,
as when he sat in a boat to gain a little distance from those
who were thronging him on the edge of the lake. Sometimes
he tells a story to his inner group of followers, the disciples,
to help them to see something in a fresh way. Sometimes it is

opponents he is addressing, such as the Pharisees or chief
priests. He told parables at dinner parties and in the Temple
precincts. Often he seems to have told a story in response to
a situation, comment or question. That is, his stories would
often not be set pieces, but told as part of a dialogue or
conversation. There was something quixotic about the
manner of this teacher who might respond to a question
about legal definition, or to a controversy about social
habits, or a request to settle a family dispute, by telling a
story. The parables – and no doubt there were more than
those recorded, and repetitions of many that are recorded –
were not sombre sermons, but sparkling repartee, part
of the cut and thrust of the human interaction of this man
on a mission.

It would be a mistake, then, to try and force the parables
into a mould, as if a single key would unlock their purpose.
The story form was simply a part of Jesus' style. But why?
One of the most obvious features of a story is that it is an
indirect form of speech. As a means of communication it
invites listeners into its own world. It calls on them to use
their imaginations. Rather than making a simple 'point', it
sets up a range of possible emotional responses. A story
that is realistic, as Jesus' stories seem to have been, reflects
the kind of world its hearers know. Its characters connect
with the sort of people with whom they are familiar. Its plot
and denouement may therefore work on the mind and
heart in profound and powerful ways.

Serious though Jesus' sense of mission undoubtedly was,
the parables suggest a lightness of spirit, a belief that it
was often more important to make people think, to help
them to imagine another way of life, than always to spell
out a message plainly. Certainly it is misguided to think
of the parables as secret code for some kind of deliberate
revelation about Jesus' identity. It is indeed fascinating to
look back on the parables from the perspective of Christian

theology, and they can yield some very suggestive meanings in the light of what his followers came to recognize about Jesus. But the parables on the whole do not give the impression that Jesus was first of all trying to say something about *himself*.

We do well to remember, however, that Jesus' mission was being carried out in a situation of increasing danger and threat. Against this background the parables may be seen as having an ambivalent effect. On the one hand, their oblique form meant that it was difficult to pin an accusation upon him on the basis of a story. On the other hand, his stories often had a sting, which would have been sharply felt by his critics, as well as by the spellbound crowds he seemed to draw. The story form of communication therefore did not ultimately protect him. Although it is overstating the case to say, as some have said, that the parables were virtually the cause of Jesus' crucifixion, they were certainly a significant element in the path of risk and courage that eventually led there.

A mysterious passage that occurs in all the first three Gospels gives a clue as to why Jesus spoke in parables, though it has also led to misunderstandings (see Mark 4:10–12). Jesus is recorded as saying that, for those who are 'outside', that is, whose hardened attitude places them outside the sphere of God's kingdom, 'everything happens in parables'. Then a purpose for this is stated: 'that seeing they may see, and not perceive; and hearing they may hear, and not understand; lest they should turn again, and be forgiven'. This has sometimes been taken – surely in error – as indicating that Jesus did not really want people *en masse* to repent and enjoy the blessings of God's kingdom; that the parables were purely a coded message for initiates, with no intention of communicating to all and sundry. This view, however, is contradicted by the overwhelming impression from the rest of the Gospels that Jesus did indeed want, urgently, to communicate to his fellow Israelites of all kinds, including those with a hostile attitude. Nor, indeed, are most of his parables opaque: 'teasing' and 'subversive' are better words often used of them. The fact that in this same passage Jesus expresses surprise that the disciples had not understood the parable of the sower shows that a contrast between enlightened initiates and obtuse outsiders does not fit the evidence of people's actual responses to Jesus. Rather, the coming of the disciples to ask Jesus about the parable, and his subsequent explanation of it, seems to represent the natural consequence of his parabolic teaching. Those who were really interested, who were drawn somehow by the magnetism of the storyteller – as well as challenged by his other, plainer sayings – wanted to gather round to hear more. Those who remained unconcerned about Jesus and his message would, perhaps, just shrug off these little stories as the puzzling speech of an eccentric or an entertainer. The stories were a means of sifting those to whom Jesus might be able to entrust the deeper 'secrets of the kingdom of God', as he called them, from those for whom these secrets would not merely be baffling, but ammunition that might be used against Jesus.

The strange purpose clause 'that seeing they may see and not perceive ...' (Mark 4:12) is not to be taken as describing the purpose of *Jesus* so much as the mysterious purpose of *God*. Some Christians might find this distinction problematic, but in fact it makes sense. The words about seeing and not perceiving, hearing and not understanding, are a quotation from the prophet Isaiah (6:9–10). They were a part of the commission he received at his calling to be a prophet. He was told, in effect, that his prophetic words of warning would by and large fall on unreceptive ears; that the more he spoke and met resistance the more his words would only serve to settle the people in their hard-heartedness. This was interpreted as God's judgement on the people for their sin.

It seems as if Mark, and quite possibly Jesus himself, saw a similar process at work in Jesus' own activity. Jesus, like Isaiah, naturally wanted his message to be heard and understood. But the parables, with their paradoxical blend of simplicity and mystery, were seen as vehicles of communication that allowed this solemn process of divine judgement to take its course. They were invitations to those who were willing to explore further; but those who did not bother to do so were thereby further hardened.

The indirect, veiled character of this form of speech seems to have a connection with Jesus' use of the phrase 'Son of Man'. This was an oblique form of self-reference which connected him to a figure in a Jewish vision, recorded in the book of Daniel, chapter 7. The 'Son of Man' in the vision, introduced in verse 13, represented the Jewish people (verse 22) and was given ultimate authority by God (verse 14). This figure had particular resonance for Jesus, for at the time of the vision the Jewish people were suffering persecution. The 'Son of Man' represented their emergence from this suffering into glorious vindication by God. Jesus used the term 'Son of Man' especially in connection with his own forebodings of suffering. There is therefore a link in mood between the obliqueness of this self-reference and the obliqueness of the parables. They are more than sharp and stinging tales: a shadow hangs over them, an ironic self-awareness.

But to say more about these stories, their purpose and effect, we must now turn to look at them one by one.

3

Rough Terrain

The Sower, Seed and Soils: Mark 4:1–20
(see also Matthew 13:3–23; Luke 8:4–15)

Again he began to teach beside the sea. Such a very large crowd gathered around him that he got into a boat on the sea and sat there, while the whole crowd was beside the sea on the land. He began to teach them many things in parables, and in his teaching he said to them: 'Listen! A sower went out to sow. And as he sowed, some seed fell on the path, and the birds came and ate it up. Other seed fell on rocky ground, where it did not have much soil, and it sprang up quickly, since it had no depth of soil. And when the sun rose, it was scorched; and since it had no root, it withered away. Other seed fell among thorns, and the thorns grew up and choked it, and it yielded no grain. Other seed fell into good soil and brought forth grain, growing up and increasing and yielding thirty and sixty and a hundredfold.' And he said, 'Let anyone with ears to hear listen!' When he was alone, those who were around him along with the twelve asked him about the parables. And he said to them, 'To you has been given the secret of the kingdom of God, but for those outside, everything comes in parables; in order that "they may indeed look, but not perceive, and may indeed listen, but not understand; so that they may not turn again and be forgiven." ' And he said to them, 'Do you not understand this parable? Then how will you understand all the parables? The sower sows the word. These are the ones on the path where the word is sown: when they hear, Satan immediately comes and takes away the word that is sown in them. And these are the ones sown on rocky ground: when they hear the word, they immediately receive it with joy. But they have no root, and endure only for a while; then, when trouble or persecution arises on account of the word, immediately they fall away. And others are those sown among the thorns: these are the ones who hear the word, but the cares of the world, and the lure of wealth, and the desire for other things come in and choke the word, and it yields nothing. And these are the ones sown on the good soil: they hear the word and accept it and bear fruit, thirty and sixty and a hundredfold.'

The land was the Jewish people's most priceless possession. Indeed, it could be said of them, as of many other peoples, that the land did not so much belong to them; they belonged to it. They believed it had been given to them by God. This was what, at heart, made their subjugation in this period by the Romans so painful. But the land was not only the tangible and treasured symbol of faith, identity and tradition. It was the key to their survival, in a way difficult to imagine for many in the industrial and post-industrial world today.

This story is strangely stark in its everyday simplicity. Mark describes how Jesus, when he told it, was in a boat on the lake, addressing a crowd 'on the land'. And it is the *land*, all around, that is the subject of the story: the land of promise, the land on which most of Jesus' fellow Israelites worked to eke out a living. It is a story about their immediate environment, about the earth that sustained their life and demanded their constant labour. It is a story, too, calculated to evoke memories and dreams of a land of freedom and plenty.

Jesus pictures a peasant farmer who went out to sow seed. This farmer, however, did not have a neatly dug seed bed in which to sow. It seems as if his plot included much rough terrain. Rather than seeking out a good patch, he sowed indiscriminately, with inevitably mixed results. One seed (this is probably the correct translation, rather than 'some') fell along the path, and the birds came and ate it up. Another seed fell on rocky ground, and though it had enough earth to germinate, it did not have the depth to sustain it when the sun got too hot. Another fell among thorns, which stifled its growth. Some, however, did find a good home, and the grain that resulted bore an ample quantity of seeds: food for that year, with plenty for planting the next. And there – apart from the pregnant words 'Let the one who has ears to hear, hear' – the story ends.

Christians are accustomed, understandably, to reading the story through the lens of the 'interpretation' that the three Gospel writers go on to record. We seldom stop to imagine what sense the hearers would have made of the story itself. Most of them, according to the Gospels, would not have heard the 'interpretation' that Jesus is recorded as giving to the disciples alone. So what would they have been left with? What could they have been expected to 'hear' in the story? What might Jesus have wanted to suggest to them or provoke in them?

When we stop to consider this we are brought up short by the ordinariness of the scene the story depicts. What possible significance could this everyday tale possess? Though some scholars have thought that the yield of the seed in the good soil is extraordinary in scale, and thus a means of hinting at divine power unusually at work, most would not regard it as completely abnormal. Similarly, there has been debate over the sower's practice of sowing over all kinds of ground. Some have argued that it was the practice in Palestine to sow before ploughing, and that

therefore the rough ground would be dug up in due course
– in other words, that this peasant farmer's behaviour
was quite normal. Others have disputed this, considering
that the farmer's action was bizarre, and therefore clearly
points to a metaphorical meaning.

What seems seldom to have been imagined is the resonance of the story with the social and economic conditions
of contemporary Palestine. With the wealthy overlords
buying up more and more land, the small, native farmers
would have been driven to the edge – literally and meta-
phorically. They would have been forced to sow where they
could, on the margins of the land, in the rough ground,
wherever they might find a good patch between stones and
weeds that would support a crop. The imaginary sower in
Jesus' story could therefore have been one of his hearers.
This was exactly the position they were in. They would be
able to identify precisely with him. Some, no doubt, were
luckier, some less so, but they would have recognized themselves and their situation. A good or poor yield of grain was
a matter of life or death.

But what then? The literary critic M. H. Abrams wrote
that literature can be both 'mirror' and 'lamp'. Was the
story simply a 'mirror' to enable the hearers to see more
clearly what was going on? It is a valuable function of
art and literature to hold a mirror up to life, to give us a
fresh perspective on the familiar. But in its brevity and
simplicity there is not much possibility in this story of a
fresh perspective. It has been argued, with reference to some
other parables, that Jesus was engaged in an exercise of
empowerment, enabling the oppressed simply to name their
oppression, as a first stage in countering it. Maybe that
partly describes his purpose here. But could there have been
something of the 'lamp' about this story as well – something
in it to guide, prompt, help; something to suggest a specific
action or response? Do we have any clues?

Let us stay with the evocative picture of the *land*. For the people of Israel, the land was not just the indispensable source of ongoing life. It was a sacred gift and trust from God. And in their Scriptures there were many promises and warnings concerning the land. Following the path of obedience to God's law would lead to rich blessing, abundant harvests. Turning to idolatry and immorality, forgetting that the land was a gift and treating it as a possession over which they had sole control, would lead to various kinds of desolation: the ravages of enemies, drought, locusts or thorns. For Israel, it was deep in the psyche that what happened to the land was a reflection of the state of their relationship with the Lord to whom they owed allegiance – even though their problem was precisely that often, at the conscious level, they forgot this.

Against this background, Jesus' story is interesting, for it hints at a complex picture. It does not reflect a situation where the land was completely desolate, and thus a bleak, unambiguous testament to God's judgement. But nor does it reflect a situation of unalloyed prosperity. Rather, it seems accurately to reflect how things were in the time of Jesus. Israel was under the domination of a foreign power; Israelites were partly alienated from the sacred land. They had to sow in the roughage if they were to have any hope of finding a propitious patch. Yet such patches were there; the harvests did come.

So the story was certainly a 'mirror'. But by drawing attention to the state of the land, which had always been a kind of barometer of God's blessing, maybe it was also a 'lamp' in a twofold sense. On the one hand, it drew attention to the difficulty of cultivation. Alienation from the land that was a vivid symbol of estrangement from God – a symbol graphically evident not only in Israel's history of exile, but in her primal myth of Eden, in which the first humans were expelled from the garden and condemned to hard labour on the land. It could thus remind people of their sacred duty to their Lord, of the importance of obedience. On the other hand, it pointed to the signs of God's continued blessing. It could thus hint that he had not abandoned them. The continuing presence of good soil is a sign of hope.

These hints were precisely that. For whatever reason, Jesus did not want at that point to spell out the message any further. He preferred to call people to listen, to think over what he said. That, apparently, was how he thought the message would sink in. Because he was not explicit, it behoves us in turn to be cautious. We should not think that we have 'caught' the meaning even though we may believe we have started to hear the kind of echoes Jesus' listeners heard. We should pause at this moment of its understated suggestiveness, and listen ourselves.

If we do so, however, we may indeed glimpse the paradox that Jesus saw in Israel's situation. Caring for the land was hard for the Israelite farmer: implicitly, repentance was called for, so that abundant blessing might again follow. Yet signs of the blessing were already there: it was possible to glimpse God's rule over his own land. And somehow the signs of blessing were themselves a further incentive to repentance. We might say that the two-handed suggestion of the parable is parallel to the two-pronged summary of Jesus' proclamation that Mark gives us: the kingdom of God is at hand – so repent.

How, then, do we account for the 'interpretation' that Jesus is recorded as giving for this parable, in private, to his disciples? This interpretation seems to move away from the parable's evocation of the situation of Israel's land by a metaphorical identification of the seed as the 'word': 'The sower sows the word.' The fate of the different seeds in the story is linked to the course of different groups of people:

those who variously have the word snatched away from them at an early stage by Satan; those who have no root and therefore fall away from faith under persecution; those who are choked by the 'thorns' of worldly care, wealth and desire; and those who hear the word, accept it, and bear fruit.

Frequently, this interpretation has been used as the framework for contemporary application of the story, and in such a way that the story itself is lost sight of. In particular, preachers and others have gone beyond both story and interpretation to offer a more detailed, supposedly neater 'allegorical' schema – that is, one in which the 'meaning' of the different elements can by ticked off point by point. If the seed is the 'word', the reasoning goes, then those who hear the word must be identified with the different types of terrain. This leads, if the logic is followed through, to a very fatalistic picture of human response to the word. Earth cannot change its character! Rocks and weeds cannot suddenly become fertile soil, or vice versa. And if such a picture is taken as the 'meaning' of the parable it becomes purely a static portrayal of a supposedly unchangeable human nature. While such a portrayal may have served as bleak but realistic assurance to the early Christians that the success or otherwise of their mission – spreading the 'word' of Jesus – was ultimately outside their control, it is hard to locate a parable with such a 'meaning' in the ministry of Jesus himself. This, no doubt, is one reason why many have considered it impossible that Jesus spoke anything like this interpretation himself. The tones of challenge and hope for change can be heard, even if obliquely, in the *story*, but the *interpretation* – on this reading – presents the disobedience of many as an irreversible *fait accompli*.

However, this reading of the interpretation given in the Gospels is misguided. Careful attention to it reveals that it does *not* press the parable into a neat allegorical schema.

The hearers of the word are *not* identified with the different
types of soil. Rather – and this may seem puzzling at first –
they are identified with the *seeds*, and thus with the word
itself. Look at the phrasing: These are the ones by the way-
side, where the word is sown ... These are the ones sown on
the rocky places ... And others are those sown among the
thorns ... And these are the ones sown upon the good
ground. The very impossibility of fitting this language into a
tidy scheme whereby seed = word and soils = people shows
that the fatalistic reading is a false trail. The interpretation
is not teaching the immutability of human nature. It is
pointing to the variety of human response, to be sure, but in
a way that draws out the challenge of the story rather than
closing it down. Hearers of the interpretation would surely
not have understood, or been intended to understand,
that there was no point in human efforts of obedience:
that they could sink either into despair as the poor soil or
complacency as the good.

Our hearing of the story itself started with the land and its
situation of exploitation by alien rulers. It ended with the
hint that the portrayal of this situation in a simple story
might well have raised the question: why? And the answer,
we suggested, would have been drawn from the ancient
tradition: the state of the sacred land reflects the state of the
sacred people. The implied message was therefore more
than a reflection of social realities. It was a summons to
human wills to repent but also to hope. It is this summons
to human wills that is continued and spelled out in the
interpretation. It involves a shift of focus from the story:
whereas the story evokes the land and its tillage in a literal
way, the interpretation uses seed as a metaphor, both for
'word' and for 'people'. Such shifts are natural in a living
oral culture, in which speech is vivid and fluid, and images
can quickly be used first one way, then another. Traces of

such a phenomenon can still be found in the way that stories, jokes or other illustrative material can go the rounds of sermons and speeches but be given a different twist or context on each occasion. Moreover, the connection between 'seed' and both 'word' and 'people' was an old one, found in the Scriptures.

Whether or not, then, the interpretation originated with Jesus himself, there is a continuity traceable between story and interpretation. What the story left as an understated hint, the interpretation draws out with a fresh use of the story's imagery. There is blessing in store for God's land and God's people, and the signs of it are already evident. But the people should ponder the reason why they are being driven to the edges of the land. Is it because they themselves have become choked or parched seeds, neglecting the word of God, which had called them into being and given them life?

4

Agricultural Sabotage

The Wheat and the Darnel:
Matthew 13:24–30, 36–43

He put before them another parable: 'The kingdom of heaven may be compared to someone who sowed good seed in his field; but while everybody was asleep, an enemy came and sowed weeds among the wheat, and then went away. So when the plants came up and bore grain, then the weeds appeared as well. And the slaves of the householder came and said to him, "Master, did you not sow good seed in your field? Where, then, did these weeds come from?" He answered, "An enemy has done this." The slaves said to him, "Then do you want us to go and gather them?" But he replied, "No; for in gathering the weeds you would uproot the wheat along with them. Let both of them grow together until the harvest; and at harvest time I will tell the reapers, Collect the weeds first and bind them in bundles to be burned, but gather the wheat into my barn." '

Then he left the crowds and went into the house. And his disciples approached him, saying, 'Explain to us the parable of the weeds of the field.' He answered, 'The one who sows the good seed is the Son of Man; the field is the world, and the good seed are the children of the kingdom; the weeds are the children of the evil one, and the enemy who sowed them is the devil; the harvest is the end of the age, and the reapers are angels. Just as the weeds are collected and burned up with fire, so will it be at the end of the age. The Son of Man will send his angels, and they will collect out of his kingdom all causes of sin and all evildoers, and they will throw them into the furnace of fire, where there will be weeping and gnashing of teeth. Then the righteous will shine like the sun in the kingdom of their Father. Let anyone with ears listen!'

The land, which formed the main subject of the first story, is also central here. The same background of hardship and tension in its cultivation is to be assumed. There are, however, two significant differences between the two situations. Whereas in the first the social source of hardship was not referred to, in this tale there is clear evidence of an 'enemy'. And whereas in the first it is the activity of a peasant farmer that is the focus, in this one it is rivalry between landowners. The man here who 'sowed' good seed in his field has slaves: presumably therefore he 'caused the seed to be sown' rather than going out with it himself.

Another difference is the prefacing of this story with the words 'The kingdom of heaven is like ...'. The occurrence of this preface in a number of parables is not to be taken as marking them out sharply from those that lack it. In a general way, it seems that the theme of God's kingdom ('heaven' was a reverential way of avoiding the name of God) underlay much of what Jesus said. The reference to the kingdom does not, however, help us greatly in imagining how the first hearers would have been struck by the story, for there is no record of Jesus spelling out *in what way* God's kingdom is like the situation of the story. This vagueness is seen in the almost rough-and-ready way that the preface is constructed: 'the kingdom of God is like a man ...'. Clearly *man* and *kingdom* are not in fact the direct points of comparison: it is left to us to discern the way in which the story reflects the nature of God's kingdom. It is quite likely that Matthew himself introduced this preface linking a number of parables with God's kingdom, since it occurs most often in his Gospel.

Like the first story, in any case, it is surely important to imagine the scene portrayed before we jump to conclusions about what it would originally have 'meant'. There is, in this instance also, an 'interpretation' of the parable, which was purportedly given in private to the disciples by Jesus. This interpretation, as we shall see, makes some explicit identifications between elements in the story and elements in the universal purposes of God. But, as with the story of the peasant farmer, we should not assume that these identifications would have been made by the crowds who first heard Jesus tell the story, or indeed that Jesus intended them to be made at that point. The interpretation should be seen more as an imaginative metaphorical development of the story's theme, whether by Jesus or his early followers.

The landowner, then, had good seed sown in his field. But at night his enemy (probably implying 'his enemy's servants') came and sowed darnel, a weed, among the wheat that had been sown. Such acts of economic sabotage were not unknown, though the motive here is not clear – perhaps it was simply a personal vendetta. When the shoots began to appear, the sabotage became apparent. The landowner's servants, the tenants, report to the master. In a vivid little piece of dialogue they appear puzzled (why are the weeds there?) and the master immediately jumps to the right conclusion (an enemy has done this). No doubt we are to assume that he was well aware that he had enemies.

The instant response of the servants is to suggest that they uproot the weeds. The landowner, however, is wiser. He knows that it will be very difficult, if not impossible, not to damage the good crop if they try to weed out the darnel at this stage. Only when both crops were fully grown could they be safely separated, the wheat stored, and the darnel burned. So he tells the servants to wait till harvest time. There the story ends.

There was no need, apparently, to say more: Jesus' audience would have recognized the landowner's command as good sense. Whether or not the servants obeyed his instructions, whether or not there was a good harvest, whether or not the separation was successfully carried out in the end, were obviously immaterial to the story. As it stands, the story acted as a 'mirror' to well-known features of agricultural life: personal rivalries; difficulty in distinguishing between good plants and bad; the wisdom of allowing them both to grow together. There would have been nothing surprising here. We might even think that such a story was trivial and inconsequential. Might there, though, be reasons for thinking that this story, like the previous one, acted as 'lamp' as well as 'mirror'?

Although the main actor in this story is a landowner with slaves, not a peasant such as those who would have mainly made up Jesus' audience, the prosperity of tenant farmers as well as slaves would have been intimately bound up with that of their landlord. If the crop was spoiled, the landlord's income would suffer, but the chances were that his dependants would feel the pinch more than he did. Thus the story treated issues that would have been of deep concern to Jesus' hearers. It could, then, have functioned as a 'lamp' in a way similar to the previous story. In picturing the familiar realities of human rivalry, and the threat of hunger through agricultural sabotage, it would again have provoked reflection on the reasons why this situation had come about.

Why was the land now a contested arena, in which individual plots must be jealously guarded, and wheat must often be painstakingly separated from weeds? What had happened to God's promises of abundant blessing? Like the previous story of the peasant farmer, this one may have recalled to Jesus' hearers the necessary conditions for God's blessing, and prompted thought about the direction their lives were taking. Yet this is also a hopeful tale. It assumes that there will be a harvest; that the landowner's advice is right; that there will be – or at least can be – a successful separation of wheat and weeds. It reminds the audience that, even in the stressful conditions of their existence, God is still giving harvests, and that there are ways of wisdom that will ensure that those harvests are not jeopardized. Moreover, it is significant that it is the landowner who knows this way of wisdom. If there are any implications here about the relationship of slaves to landlords, they are certainly not that tenants should try to improve their lot by seeking independence and rebelling against their masters. Rather, the picture is one in which sufficiency for them depends upon their co-operation with their masters, who (at least in this case) appear better skilled in agricultural techniques than they are. This is historically plausible, given various treatises on agriculture in Roman literature.

This story, then, like the earlier one, may be heard as hinting both at the reality of God's blessing in the midst of the people's oppression, and the challenge of returning to a whole-hearted obedience. It adds the interesting extra picture of co-operation between slaves and master. The theme of co-operation as opposed to confrontation with the controlling figures in society is to swell louder as we read further stories.

The interpretation of the story develops it in a more colourful way than in the case of the parable of the sower, seed and soils. Again, however, we may see a profound continuity between story and interpretation. In this case, the presence of good and evil side by side in the whole situation evoked by the story – the possibility of a harvest in the midst of struggle and toil – is focused down, in the interpretation, on a vivid contrast between the good seed as representing 'the sons of the kingdom' and the darnel as representing 'the sons of the evil one'. The sower of the wheat is the 'Son of Man' (that mysterious self-designation of Jesus); the enemy is the devil. The harvest, in accordance with imagery from the Old Testament, is 'the end of the age', the time of reckoning at the climax of the present world order. The reapers are the angels who carry out the Son of Man's bidding, gathering out and burning 'all causes of sin and all evildoers' from the field, which is the world.

The differentiation here between 'sons of the kingdom' and 'sons of the evil one' may imply to our ears that people are either one or the other, without any choice, or opportunity to change. This, however, is to misunderstand the Semitic idiom that lies behind the phrases. They describe character rather than indicating origin. Like our English expression 'he really is his father's son' – indicating a strong and telling likeness of character or appearance – 'son of' here points to *likeness* rather than stressing parentage. The 'sons of the kingdom' are those who live in kingdom ways; the 'sons of the evil one' are those who do not. The emphasis of the interpretation is not that people are fixed in these categories, but that evil will ultimately be rooted out from God's world. There is thus an implied imperative of obedience, as in the story itself. Conversely, there is here too an explicit promise: 'the righteous shall shine like the sun in the kingdom of their Father'. This rather beautifully echoes the theme of the story that, one day, wheat and weeds will be clearly distinguishable. The righteous will be seen as such in the day of the 'harvest'.

The interpretation makes no mention of the central element in the story, the inclination of the servants to up-root the weeds too early. This suggests that we should see it

not as a strict account of the story's intended 'meaning' but
rather a further development or re-orienting of its focus.
The story's elements have been given a metaphorical meaning, and the main stress is on the fact of ultimate judgement,
not the inclination to separate good and evil before the time
is right. This development is drawn especially from Hebrew
prophetic expectation. The 'harvest' was a familiar term for
judgement, found in Joel 3:13. To 'gather out' was a term
for the separation of the righteous from the wicked. The
picture of fire, connected of course with the burning of
the darnel in the story, seems (along with weeping and
gnashing) to have been a current Jewish way of evoking the
terrors of ultimate punishment, which is a characteristic
theme of Matthew. The image of the righteous 'shining like
the sun' is taken from Daniel 12:3. Here too it is interesting
to see the connection with the story, for those who shine in
Daniel 12 are in fact the 'wise', and it is especially *wisdom*
rather than righteousness that is prominent in the story
(though in biblical terms the two are intimately bound up).

Two further features of the interpretation are worth
noting. The sower is identified as 'the Son of Man'. This is a
more explicit identification than in the interpretation of the
previous story, where the sower is more vaguely identified
as any one who sows 'the word of God'. In the thinking of
Jesus or the early church such a 'sower' might be understood (in various contexts) as Jesus, a disciple, or God
himself. Here, by contrast, the use of the phrase 'Son of
Man' reflects the atmosphere of intense expectation drawn
from the Jewish visionary language that we have noted. As
we saw in Chapter 2, the 'Son of Man' was a figure in the
vision recorded in Daniel 7 to whom the God of Israel had
given great authority, and the expression was used as a form
of oblique self-reference by Jesus himself.

The implication of its use here is clear. The 'sons of the
kingdom', who are the 'good seed' sown by the 'Son of

Man', are those who have responded to the message of Jesus. This seems to indicate that the interpretation as a whole comes from early Christian reflection. The church soon recognized Jesus as the ultimate judge of what was good and evil, so 'good seed' could be interpreted not only as those who were obedient to God, but more specifically as those who followed Jesus. Further, the kingdom is seen in verse 41 as the *Son of Man's* kingdom, not only God's.

The other feature to remark upon is the description of what, and who, is 'gathered out of' God's kingdom. Whereas the initial identification of the darnel is simply with 'the sons of the evil one', it is said that the angels sent by the Son of Man will 'gather out of his kingdom *all causes of sin*, and all who do wickedness'. This implies a more radical uprooting of evil, not merely punishment of the wicked; thus even within the interpretation there is a development from one 'meaning' of the darnel to a broader one.

So, from a story that evoked an aspect of the tension in contemporary peasant life, hinting both at the need for obedience to the God of the harvest and the reality of his continued blessing in tandem with wise human action, the 'interpretation' emerges as a vivid metaphorical expansion, drawing on Scriptural imagery to reinforce the certainty of ultimate judgement. The continuity between story and interpretation is found not in consistency of detail but in the fundamental orientation to both challenge and hope. Story and interpretation alike, though in very different degrees of directness, point to the gift of God to his faithful and wise people, and his summons to obedience.

5

Dangerous Journey

The Good Samaritan:
Luke 10:25–37

Just then a lawyer stood up to test Jesus. 'Teacher,' he said, 'what must I do to inherit eternal life?' He said to him, 'What is written in the law? What do you read there?' He answered, 'You shall love the Lord your God with all your heart, and with all your soul, and with all your strength, and with all your mind; and your neighbor as yourself.' And he said to him, 'You have given the right answer; do this, and you will live.' But wanting to justify himself, he asked Jesus, 'And who is my neighbor?' Jesus replied, 'A man was going down from Jerusalem to Jericho, and fell into the hands of robbers, who stripped him, beat him, and went away, leaving him half dead. Now by chance a priest was going down that road; and when he saw him, he passed by on the other side. So likewise a Levite, when he came to the place and saw him, passed by on the other side. But a Samaritan while travelling came near him; and when he saw him, he was moved with pity. He went to him and bandaged his wounds, having poured oil and wine on them. Then he put him on his own animal, brought him to an inn, and took care of him. The next day he took out two denarii, gave them to the innkeeper, and said, "Take care of him; and when I come back, I will repay you whatever more you spend."

Which of these three, do you think, was a neighbor to the man
who fell into the hands of the robbers?' He said, 'The one who
showed him mercy.' Jesus said to him, 'Go and do likewise.'

The road from Jerusalem down to Jericho, in the south of
Palestine, was seventeen miles long, and it crossed rugged
and dangerous terrain. What sort of man might it be who
was walking it in this story of Jesus? We do not know. He is
simply 'a certain man'. Perhaps that is the point: it does not
matter who he is – he could be anyone. Again, it seems,
Jesus is telling a tale of everyday life. Then, as now, and
throughout human history, people have travelled for many
different reasons.

Palestine in the time of Jesus, tense under Roman rule,
had more than its fair share of brigands. The robbers who
made this particular route notorious were there as usual.
They fell upon the traveller, stripped him of his clothing and
no doubt anything of worth that was concealed within it,
assaulted him sufficiently that he would not be able to give
chase or raise the alarm, and left him half dead. Perhaps
indeed they thought he *was* dead. It is another detail we are
left to wonder about.

The now-wounded man was not, however, the only
traveller on the road that day. A priest came along. There
would have been priests going to and from Jerusalem on a
regular basis. They were people of status and would have
ridden on beasts of burden. They fulfilled duties in the
Temple according to a rota system, but mostly lived outside
the city in villages or towns. We do not know which way
this priest was going. If he was heading towards Jerusalem
one of the concerns uppermost in his mind would have been
to keep himself ritually pure so as to be able to perform his
Temple duties. If he contracted 'impurity' – for instance
through contact with a dead body – there would have been a
long and tedious process of ritual cleansing to go through.

He would perhaps miss the high point of his year, his tour of duty in the sacred precincts. If, on the other hand, he was returning home after his temple duties it would equally have been a great inconvenience to have had to return and undergo the rituals of cleansing. Maybe this was why he passed by the injured man without stopping to investigate.

However, we do not know whether Jesus' hearers – the lawyer in Luke's narrative to whom the story is directly addressed, or other bystanders – would have assumed that to be the reason. Maybe they knew that the priest would have been cautious for another reason: since the wounded man was naked and unconscious no one would be able to tell by his speech or his dress what sort of person he was or where he came from. The wisdom writer Jesus ben Sirach, writing a couple of centuries before Jesus of Nazareth lived (in the book also known as 'Ecclesiasticus'), had warned that one should know the person one is helping, lest one be found to be aiding 'sinners' (Sirach 12:1–7). A scrupulous priest might have been reluctant to help one who might turn out to be a Gentile, or in some other way tarred with the brush of being a 'sinner'.

Or maybe Jesus' hearers simply recognized familiar human nature at work: revulsion at disfigured flesh; aversion to death; a pretence to oneself that one has not noticed; fear for one's own safety. And very likely they would not have been shocked at this picture of one of their spiritual leaders. Among the ordinary people the priests, on the whole, were little respected. They were seen, with justification, as being too much in league with the Roman rulers. The Temple system, with its tithes and taxes, was in its way as oppressive as the Roman regime, and closely allied to it. At any rate, the priest passed by on the other side of the road. The helpless man remained helpless.

Levites were the junior members of the priestly hierarchy who assisted in various Temple duties. A Levite came along the Jerusalem to Jericho road after the priest. Arriving at the spot where the wounded man still lay, he also, when he noticed him, did not stop, but passed by on the other side. Perhaps he knew that the priest was on the road ahead of him and took his cue from the priest's caution. The listeners would have been no more surprised at the picture of such behaviour than they would have been in the case of the priest. In both cases there might have been a wry smirk at this storyteller who didn't mind showing the priestly caste in a poor light.

Then there is a surprise. A third person is also on the road. He is not, as might have been expected from the sequence of the story so far, an 'ordinary Jew', a mere member of the public. He is one of the hated race of Samaritans. Though the Jews and Samaritans shared a common ancestry, they regarded each other with contempt. The Samaritans were feared and abhorred by the Jews, especially following a fairly recent incident in which the Jerusalem Temple had been shockingly desecrated at their hands by the scattering of human bones. Priests and Levites were not much loved, but Samaritans were loathed! No doubt the audience expected this one to show a gesture of contempt towards the wounded man, which far outstripped the blameworthy, but understandable, cowardice of the other two.

But an even greater surprise is in store. The hated Samaritan did not pass by. Rather, he was 'moved with compassion', touched with a deep pity for the helpless victim. He did not shrink from contact with him but 'came to him'. Implicit, perhaps, are courage (might he have feared that the robbers were still around?) and a readiness to disregard social enmities (would he have recognized, or assumed, the victim to be a Jew?, or was it simply a human being in a state of total vulnerability that he saw?). He then showed a quality of care that contrasted starkly with the self-distancing of his predecessors on the road: binding up the wounds; applying the standard medicaments of oil and wine; then putting the man on his own ass and taking him to the nearest inn. Nor did his attention stop there: unwilling simply to leave the man to the mercy of a possibly unreliable host (innkeepers had a very bad reputation), the Samaritan not only left the innkeeper with money to look after the man, but promised to call in again on his return and reimburse him further if necessary. The wounded man had nothing; the innkeeper would have had few scruples about exploiting his penury, that is, enslaving him; but the Samaritan would have none of that. It was a costly act in which the Samaritan risked both a hostile reception by the innkeeper and the suspicions of other travellers who might easily have believed him to be the assailant. The Samaritan's ultimate plan, we may guess, was to 'pick up' the man again when he returned past the inn and escort him back to Jerusalem. And so the story ends, with the picture of compassion shown by an enemy lingering in the hearers' imaginations.

What impact would such a story have had on those hearers? Luke records that Jesus told it to a legal expert who was testing him concerning the criterion for gaining 'eternal life', the promised age of fulfilment to which the Jews looked forward. Jesus affirms the lawyer's own view that the great necessity is summed up in two of the old commandments of the law: to love the Lord – Yahweh, Israel's God – with all one's being and one's fellow humans as oneself. The lawyer, however, wants to press the test further. In common with the Pharisees, he wants to make the application of the command more precise, and therefore the command itself more manageable, easy to keep. So he asks Jesus 'who is my neighbour?'

The story constitutes Jesus' answer. For the lawyer, and the knot of other listeners who were no doubt gathered round, the shock and strangeness of this answer would have been considerable. For one thing, it appears not to be a direct answer to the question. Jesus says nothing to define, either exclusively or inclusively, who one's 'neighbour' is. Rather he pictures for his hearers what loving one's neighbour means in practice. But he does far more than this, for the example of neighbourliness he sets before them is a person who, on account of his race, would never have been seen by a Jewish audience as one to imitate. The question Jesus puts to the lawyer at the end – which of these three *proved to be* a neighbour to the one who fell among the robbers? – stands the lawyer's own question on its head. The apparent reluctance of the lawyer even to call the Samaritan a Samaritan in his answer tells its own story. Jesus' tale has pictured a world in which people of true love – and therefore people who will inherit 'eternal life' – are not confined to one particular nation, no matter how conscious such a nation may be of being 'chosen'. It has portrayed an unclean enemy as a pattern to be imitated and the guardians of Jewish purity, the priest and the Levite, as unreliable guides. The lawyer, and the other listeners, must go and do as the Samaritan had done.

Can we capture both the reticence and the needling sharpness of what Jesus was doing here? He gave the lawyer both less and more than he was seeking. Less, because Jesus refused to play his game of legal definition. Instead, his answer took the form of a story, giving a glimpse of a possibility, not a prescription or a rule. More, because Jesus addressed not the lesser question of whom one should love, but the greater question of who *is able* to love, and therefore who is able to enter the life of the age to come. The lesser question, motivated by the desire for assurance that the command was safely manageable, is shown up as unworthy. The greater question, for nationalists under pressure from an alien power, would have been taboo. But it was precisely the refusal to countenance it that Jesus seems to have discerned behind the lawyer's inquiry.

In the figure of the Samaritan Jesus paints a picture of true humanity. There are no extraordinary feats of heroism here: like the victim, he is an ordinary person. In that ordinariness Jesus made him an example capable of being followed. But in making him a Samaritan he subverts his hearers' view of who may keep God's law, who is within the pale, who is able to love. 'Oil and wine' were elements essential to the priestly sacrifices offered in the Temple, but here an unclean half-caste is seen as offering the true sacrifice of compassion – a quality seen in the Old Testament as issuing from the heart of God himself. The enemy despised because of his race or his adherence to a different tradition of law may be the very one to teach true obedience.

6

Storage Space

The Rich Fool:
Luke 12:13–21

Someone in the crowd said to him, 'Teacher, tell my brother to divide the family inheritance with me.' But he said to him, 'Friend, who set me to be a judge or arbitrator over you?' And he said to them, 'Take care! Be on your guard against all kinds of greed; for one's life does not consist in the abundance of possessions.' Then he told them a parable: 'The land of a rich man produced abundantly. And he thought to himself, "What should I do, for I have no place to store my crops?" Then he said, "I will do this: I will pull down my barns and build larger ones, and there I will store all my grain and my goods. And I will say to my soul, 'Soul, you have ample goods laid up for many years; relax, eat, drink, be merry.'" But God said to him, "You fool! This very night your life is being demanded of you. And the things you have prepared, whose will they be?" So it is with those who store up treasures for themselves but are not rich toward God.'

From time to time the Gospels give us a vivid account of an individual exchange between a person and Jesus. In such incidents, like this one in which a man in the crowd asks him to use his authority to settle a property dispute, we get a glimpse of the way that Jesus' message touched ordinary people – often in a manner they were not seeking.

Jesus' response to the man was rather severe. The division of property was a serious matter, and we may guess that the man was from a family grown too large for a meagre plot of land to be divided any further. The only option for someone effectively disinherited in this way might be to seek a living in the highly insecure and seasonal day-labouring job market, or to resort to begging. Yet Jesus refuses to adjudicate in the dispute. With characteristic penetration, he sees at the heart of the man's request not so much the danger of starvation as the danger of greed. 'Take heed, and beware of all covetousness': 'life' is not defined by the quantity of one's possessions.

'True', one can imagine the man thinking, 'but everyone needs *something* to live on.' But Jesus, in the story he then proceeds to tell, persists with the issue of greed. The story is a warning against aspiring to be like the wealthy, who only hoard their wealth for themselves, instead of sharing it for the common good. It is also a graphic account of precisely why the questioner finds himself in his current parlous state. The fruits of the land, and the land itself, were increasingly accruing to the wealthy few, and ebbing away from the impoverished majority. The problem, Jesus implies, is not one that can be sorted out simply by dividing a small patrimony into ever-smaller portions. Even if the man's brother were to accept Jesus' authority, this would not change the fundamental cancer in Israel's life, the injustice that refused a decent living to many. Only a change of heart by the grasping rich could effect that, and such a change of heart no teacher, not even Jesus, could enforce.

In the figure of the 'rich man' in the story, Jesus may have intended his hearers to imagine one of the Roman over-lords, or one of the small élite, Jewish or Gentile, who were their lackeys. Such people bought up more and more of the land so that many of the traditional peasant farmers, who technically became their tenants, ended up as virtual slaves. One year, the extensive lands of this rich man gave an excellent harvest. The story then focuses on the man's thought processes – a vivid touch seen in several of Jesus' parables recorded by Luke. We see him planning. He does not have enough storage space for his bumper crop. One possibility would have been large-scale distribution to his tenants, but this does not seem to have entered his head. His instinct is to pull down his barns and build bigger ones.

It is the next step in his internal reasoning that is really revealing. He wants the security he believes will come from the possession of such a large quantity of grain. Grain would keep for a good many years. Not only would it provide for him and his family; it could be sold at a profit when he wished, for ready cash. A small class of people at the top of the pile enjoyed a luxurious lifestyle and that is precisely what this man plans for. Notice how his self-centredness is seen not only in his lack of consideration for others, but in his self-absorbed inner dialogue: 'And I will say to my soul, "Soul, you have many goods laid up for many years; take your ease, eat, drink, be merry." ' It hints, perhaps, at a basically lonely man whose avarice has left him with no one but himself to talk to. It is interesting to contrast this with the more hopeful picture of masters and servants discussing plans with each other, which we see in some other stories (see Chapters 4 and 7).

Then comes the shock. The man is not, after all, alone in his thoughts. God (in a rare direct appearance in Jesus' stories) speaks to him and calls him a fool. 'Fool' was more than a term of casual abuse. The fool in Israelite understanding was one who lived life without reference to God. That is precisely the pose in which this brief tale captures this rich man. In biblical terms, to fail to seek justice and compassion is to fail to know God. But to be foolish was also, in a very practical sense, to ignore one's own best interests. 'Wisdom' was the way of common sense, the way to true life. And this man was foolish because he had failed to reckon up where true life lay. He had not seen that life does not consist in the abundance of possessions. He had spent his 'life' in a fixation of acquisitiveness and had missed out on life itself in the process. His tragedy was not that God was now asking for his 'soul' in death: his tragedy was that he had not had life while he could. He had imagined himself master of his destiny, the 'owner' of all he 'possessed'. Now comes the penetrating word reminding him that in fact he had *owned* nothing. Even his 'soul' was on loan, now summoned back by the lender. Now, inevitably, all he had stored up for himself *would* pass to others. His dreams of longevity and security had proved illusory. 'So', says Jesus, 'is the one who lays up treasure for himself, and is not rich towards God' – 'richness towards God' being a way of speaking about generosity to one's neighbour.

In the context of Jesus' response to the questioner, the story is a reminder that wealth offers no ultimate security. The temptation to think that it does can beguile the poor as readily as the rich – and any in between. Dreams of a prosperous (or an even more prosperous) future may, in fact, so preoccupy a person's mind that not only is there the ever-present threat of crushing disillusionment – most notably through the arrival of death itself – but the fact that they also miss out on the life that God is giving in the present. We ought not to overlook the difficulty of this message for the truly poor or its challenge for the rich. The call to both is to wake up to the reality that neither life nor safety are found in great possessions.

But if this sounds stark and bleak, there is a hopeful aura to the parable too, when heard in its social setting. It says that God is in charge. Grasping landowners do not have it all their own way, notwithstanding appearances. There is not one of them who is not subject to the common lot of all humanity – death. Death, the supreme and ever-present pointer to human finitude, is also the remover of tyrants and oppressors, and so becomes God's merciful agent for those who suffer at their hands.

Moreover, as with all Jesus' stories, this one is not closed. It speaks of death with the overtones of God's calling us to account, but it does not pass final judgement on any individual or class of people. The kingdom is near, but that brings the *possibility* of repentance, not its *impossibility*. Calling the rich man's planned hoarding 'folly' carries the implication that there would have been another way. It is possible for the rich, like the poor, to discover true life through the ways of justice and compassion. Other stories of Jesus picture the rich in precisely such a light: as generous to employees and retainers. Jesus was not propounding a form of egalitarian society or some unrealistic Utopian ideal. Nor was he stereotyping particular groups, implying that all rich people were selfish. He was, however, realistically pointing to the beguiling dangers of wealth and calling both rich and poor to eschew them.

7

Fruit Delayed

The Barren Fig Tree:
Luke 13:6–9

Then he told this parable: 'A man had a fig tree planted in his vineyard; and he came looking for fruit on it and found none. So he said to the gardener, "See here! For three years I have come looking for fruit on this fig tree, and still I find none. Cut it down! Why should it be wasting the soil?" He replied, "Sir, let it alone for one more year, until I dig around it and put manure on it. If it bears fruit next year, well and good; but if not, you can cut it down." '

A fig tree in a vineyard would have been a common sight. In their maturity fig trees in Palestine can bear fruit for ten months of the year. Not surprisingly, the fig tree and the vine together were proverbial symbols of prosperity. Again, we have a glimpse in this little story into the life of Jesus' Palestinian neighbours – but a glimpse that was intended to stir up thought.

Why was there no fruit to be found on the fig tree when this landowner came looking for it? We can assume that he knew the normal cycle of growth. The tree would take three years to come to maturity. The law prescribed that the fruit of the first three years after that was forbidden, and that the next year's should be made an offering of praise to the Lord (Leviticus 19:23–4). But it is a moot point whether the landowner would have been a law-observant Jew. What we know of the kind of ancient society where such a scene is placed suggests that many of the ruling class were rapacious, riding roughshod over both the letter and the spirit of the law, 'joining house to house' and 'adding field to field' as in Isaiah's indictment of the oppressors of his time, some eight centuries earlier (Isaiah 5:8). It is doubtful whether the powerful in the time of Jesus were any more generally inclined to be scrupulous in the careful use of the earth and its fruits, in acknowledgement of the creator, than they are now.

That being the case, the 'three years' during which this man 'came looking' for figs may well have been those first three years when the fruit, if there had been any, would have been forbidden. But there was none to find. Once more a pregnant picture opens up of blessing withheld and a sombre hint is given of failure in the natural order. Why should it be? That surely is the question that hangs in the air. Here is another sign of the sacred land *not* bearing fruit as promised.

As in the tale of agricultural sabotage (Chapter 4) this story, though brief, comes alive because it is dramatized with dialogue. There it was a case of the labourers suggesting a course of action and the landowner wisely cautioning against it. Here it is the reverse. The landowner wants to cut down the fig tree because, if it is bearing no fruit, it is wasting space and drawing off goodness that could be feeding other figs and vines. The normal practice would have been to axe the tree at its roots and remove it completely. The labourer, however, proposes that they give it another year: he will apply a mulch of manure round the trunk and see what happens. If it still bears no fruit it can be cut down. As in the other tale, this one ends with the words of advice.

We are not told whether the servants heeded the master in the other story, or whether the master heeded the servant in this. Presumably it did not matter to the story. We are left, again, with a vivid little picture of co-operation between landlord and labourers, a sharing of wisdom for the sake of common benefit. Master and servant alike have a stake in the prosperity of the land.

At the back of both these stories, like the others told by Jesus about the land, is the harsh reality of competition for good soil. Whether for the rich who were buying out more and more plots, or the poor who were just managing to hold on to their patch, space and fertile earth were scarce and precious. The landowner's comment here is revealing: 'Why should it use up the ground?' And once more the mood of the story is tentatively hopeful. Maybe there *will* be figs next year, with careful husbandry, just as, in other tales, some seed *did* produce a bumper harvest, and the wheat might have a chance to grow to maturity even among the darnel.

Unlike the stories we looked at in Chapters 3 and 4, however, there is no 'interpretation' of this story recorded in the Gospels. But, interestingly, there are strong similarities to an incident recorded in Matthew and Mark, in which Jesus at the beginning of his last week in Jerusalem found a fruitless fig tree and cursed it (Matthew 21:18–22; Mark 11:12–14, 20–25). Without leaving behind this story he told in Luke 13, and its original, understated suggestiveness, the incident gives us the clue as to the wider significance seen by Luke, and probably by Jesus too, of the vignette of a fig tree being reprieved.

Mark records that when Jesus and his disciples were on their way from their lodging in Bethany to Jerusalem, the day after Jesus' symbolic arrival in the city riding on a donkey, Jesus was hungry. He saw a fig tree in leaf, but without fruit. Mark makes it quite explicit (uncomfortably for us, in view of what happens next!) that it was not the season for figs, so no fruit could have been expected. Thereupon Jesus pronounced a curse, saying that no one would ever eat fruit from it again.

At that point in the story we leave the fig tree and follow Jesus and the disciples into Jerusalem, where, in an act symbolic of God's purpose to restore his people and the purity of their worship, Jesus drives moneychangers out of the Temple precincts (Mark 11:15–19). However, as they pass the fig tree again the following morning, the disciples notice that it has withered. When this is pointed out to Jesus he uses it as an object lesson in the power of faith and prayer.

Through the way he has intertwined the stories of the fig tree and the Temple cleansing, Mark (who is fond of this technique) clearly suggests that the incidents interpret each other. The fig tree is like Israel, who is under a curse for her failure to bear the 'fruit' of justice and holiness – as seen in the corruption at the very heart of her life, in the Temple. The expulsion of the moneychangers from the Temple, similarly, is a graphic warning that Israel herself is under judgement. Jesus' words about the power of faith and prayer serve to reinforce the fact that these two symbolic warnings were no empty threats. They were carried out in the utter conviction that God was at that moment at work to bring his people to judgement.

The fact that 'it was not the season for figs' only emphasises the *symbolic* nature of Jesus' act: this was not an act of vengeance on a poorly performing fig tree! However, the fact that Jesus' action was prompted in the first instance by hunger reminds us that we should not drive a wedge between symbol and meaning. The spiritual state of Israel was mirrored, as we have seen, in the economic hardship and turmoil she was enduring. Like the old prophets, Jesus assumed that when people bore the fruit of justice the land would bear the fruits of the harvest. His hunger was probably not the mere slight pang that the person from a prosperous country feels as lunchtime approaches, soon to be forgotten. More likely it was the condition of many Palestinian peasants for much of the time: a constant, gnawing reminder that all was not well in the land of promise. Trees such as figs have their seasons for fruiting, but had God's people been living in God's way, hunger would have been banished all year round. So the cursing of the fig tree is far more than a mere 'illustration' of the impending fate of Israel. It can be seen as a *cri de coeur* from the hungry Jesus, who shares in his people's sufferings: may these sufferings cease!

We return to the story in Luke. It is gentler, less final, than the actual incident on the Bethany to Jerusalem road recorded by Mark and Matthew. In Jesus' story the fig tree is given one last chance. This reflects the hopeful spirit of Jesus seen especially in Luke: weeping over Jerusalem, longing that Israel might be saved even though he sees the clouds of doom lowering overhead. But the incident of the cursing sheds light on the story Jesus told. It is a reminder again that, before there can be fruit from trees, there must be fruit from people – and first of all, from those God has specially called as his vineyard, as trees planted by streams of water.

8

Family Threatened

The Prodigal Son:
Luke 15:11–32

Then Jesus said, 'There was a man who had two sons. The younger of them said to his father, "Father, give me the share of the property that will belong to me." So he divided his property between them. A few days later the younger son gathered all he had and travelled to a distant country, and there he squandered his property in dissolute living. When he had spent everything, a severe famine took place throughout that country, and he began to be in need. So he went and hired himself out to one of the citizens of that country, who sent him to his fields to feed the pigs. He would gladly have filled himself with the pods that the pigs were eating; and no one gave him anything. But when he came to himself he said, "How many of my father's hired hands have bread enough and to spare, but here I am dying of hunger! I will get up and go to my father, and I will say to him, 'Father, I have sinned against heaven and before you; I am no longer worthy to be called your son; treat me like one of your hired hands.' " So he set off and went to his father. But while he was still far off, his father saw him and was filled with compassion; he ran and put his arms around him and kissed him. Then the son said to him, "Father, I have sinned against heaven and before you; I am no longer worthy to be called your son." But the father said to his slaves, "Quickly, bring out a robe – the best one – and put it on him; put a ring on his finger and sandals on his feet. And get the fatted calf and kill it, and let us eat and celebrate; for this son of mine was dead and is alive again; he was lost and is found!" And they began to celebrate. Now his elder son was in the field; and when he came and approached the house, he heard music and dancing. He called one of the slaves and asked what was going on. He replied, "Your brother has come, and your father has killed the fatted calf, because he has got him back safe and sound." Then he became angry and refused to go in. His father came out and began to plead with him. But he answered his father, "Listen! For all these years I have been working like a slave for you, and I have never disobeyed your command; yet you have never given me even a young goat so that I might celebrate with my friends. But when this son of yours came back, who has devoured your property with prostitutes, you killed the fatted calf for him!" Then the father said to him, "Son, you are always with me, and all that is mine is yours. But we had to celebrate and rejoice, because this brother of yours was dead and has come to life; he was lost and has been found." '

One option in the stressful days in which Jesus and his fellow Palestinians lived was, naturally, to try to escape: to leave the poverty, the insecurity, the sense of living under the shadow of alien powers. If somehow one could get hold of some cash, even a modest amount, one might be able to travel and start a new life free of suffocating restrictions. There was always the chance that, elsewhere, things would be better.

This is the human situation that lies behind this tale. Yet it has often been read in more-than-human terms. The wayward son returning to his father has been seen as a graphic portrayal of any human being who returns to God from a life of self-willed indulgence. His compassionate father, likewise, is seen as the quintessential image of God himself given to us by Jesus. But to jump to these identifications too quickly is to miss much of the story and its suggestive power. First and foremost, this is the story of a human family, and all three of the members of the family we see are crucial to the story.

'There was a man …'. Like the other anonymous characters in Jesus' stories we have a sense that this could be anyone: that is the point. And yet Jesus' hearers would have gained a slightly more precise impression of him than this. This was a man of some substance. He was not one of the wealthiest – gathering his friends and neighbours together implies that he lived in a village, not isolated in a grand house on an estate. But he was not one of the poorest either. There is an inheritance to divide – enough for the younger son to give himself a wild time with his share. Later it will come out that the man had hired servants, slaves and live-stock. He was not a peasant on the breadline.

He had two sons. It was the custom for the elder son to inherit the greater part of the estate of a deceased father. Why the younger asked, before his father's death, for his share, we are not told. Perhaps Jesus' hearers would have recognized here simply the familiar signs of youthful adventure. Perhaps we are to imagine that the younger son knew that the elder would inherit the house and land, and that there would be difficulty in both of them staying there, especially when they themselves married and had families. Maybe, in uncertain times, the philosophy of 'eat, drink and be merry' in the present – like the attitude of the landowner in Jesus' story in Luke 12:16–21 – seemed the natural one to adopt. At any rate, the son's request to the father to give him his share would have sounded deeply offensive. It was a way of saying to his father 'I wish you were dead.'

The father's reaction, even at this early point in the story, is therefore highly significant. He does as his son asks, notwithstanding the warning given in the book of Sirach (33:20–24) that a father should not give away his property before he dies. That he 'divided his property between' his two sons implies that the elder received his share as well. This appears to have been the subject of some misunderstanding. Later in the story the elder son complains that his father had never even given him a goat so he could throw a party with his friends. The father responds that 'all that is mine is yours'. We may assume that the elder son continued to live respectfully with his father (and mother? – maybe she was dead; more likely she is one of the many 'hidden women' in these tales, recounted as they were in a heavily male-dominated culture). He had no wish to emulate his brother's rebellious behaviour. But this loyal son had not grasped the fact that his father was treating him, too, as grown up, indeed as an equal; that all that was the father's – the house and livestock and land and its produce, all that remained after the younger had taken his portion – was indeed his. He was still expecting to receive gifts like a child, while all along his father was entrusting him with everything that they had left, and expecting him to enjoy it freely.

How would such a father have felt when a younger son went off in such circumstances? What would it have been like for the family remaining behind? Those listening to the story would have known how vulnerable the father had allowed the entire family unit to become. He had allowed the younger son to turn his share of the precious inheritance into cash, thus diminishing the size of the family property, and to leave home without any intent of using the cash for the family's benefit. But more serious even than the writing off of this part of the inheritance was the departure of the son himself. A child, especially a son, was in this culture a priceless and extremely practical asset. Although, for the poor, too many children would have meant too many mouths to feed, children also represented the blessing of God and a source of vital support for ageing parents. Left with only one son, the family was exposed, at risk.

The father, then, has been extraordinarily acquiescent to his son's offensive actions, first in requesting his share, then in abandoning the family. What of the younger lad's behaviour now? The tale is briefly told. He threw away his newly gained wealth in an orgy of self-indulgence in a far country. What this dissolute lifestyle consisted of is left to the imagination, but Jesus' hearers would have been able to guess the kind of thing he had in mind. The older brother's mention of prostitutes later in the story shows that he, at least, had a shrewd idea of where the family treasure was heading. Other badges of luxurious living for which people craved would have included extravagant cuisine, free-flowing wine and ostentatious attire. And, crucially, he was 'in a far country' as he indulged himself. Away from the restraints not only of home but also of the law of Israel, he was free to do as he pleased.

There came, however, the dreadful moment when all was spent. To make matters worse, it coincided with a severe famine. The implications of this, presumably, would be that, whatever meagre earnings he might be able to scrape together, he would scarcely be able to afford the rocketing price of food. He had removed himself from his source of security on the family farm. Now he found himself 'joined' to a local man as a swineherd. The significance of this should not be lost on us. 'Joined' is a word for intimate association. To become the employee or, indeed, the slave – as seems almost to have been the case here – of a Gentile would have been shameful enough for a Jew. To find oneself tending pigs, unclean to the Jewish people, was more degrading still. The famine meant that there was no

employment as a day-labourer harvesting crops. Looking
after pigs was his only option. Even then, it seems his
employer had little to give him to keep body and soul
together. He was reduced to eating the bitter-tasting carob-
pods, which were fed to the pigs, and still there was an
aching hunger. From tasting the brief thrills of *nouveau
riche* luxury, he descends to tasting the fodder of unclean
animals and the bitter pill of poverty. The same words are
used of his 'longing to be filled' as are used in another story,
that of the beggar Lazarus, who is 'longing to be filled' with
crumbs from the rich man's table (Luke 16:21).

The son has in fact discovered the same lesson as was
exemplified in the story of the rich man with a bumper
harvest: that *life* does not consist in the abundance of
possessions. He has sacrificed the most vital and most basic
thing, the means of life itself, for the unnecessary, the trivial
and the immoral. From Jesus' point of view, this seems to
have been his most profound error, greater even than the
accompanying sins of rebellion, selfishness and impure
living. He had forgotten the way of wisdom, which is
the way to life itself. And the ancient world was acutely
conscious that, for *life* to be preserved and enjoyed, *mutual*
support and the bonds of community were utterly essential.
For Judaism, the justice enshrined in the Torah given
by God to Israel entailed, centrally, obedience to God,
family loyalty and care for all members of the community,
including the poorest. In demanding his inheritance,
leaving his family and spending his money on himself, this
young man had flouted all three principles. He had left
the environment where God was worshipped, where he
owed a duty to his relatives and neighbours, and where he
himself would receive support in time of need. Now he was
alone and alienated from that safe and sacred space. This
was not divine punishment for his folly, simply its self-
imposed consequence. And, in a moment of self-awareness,

he sees that there is only one course of action he can now take.

We have already seen examples of brief and telling dialogues or inner thought processes in the parables. Here now is one of the most poignant. The dejected young man recalls that even the 'hired servants' engaged by his father to work on the farm have (in his experience) always had more than enough to eat. But now he, a son of the family, is literally dying of hunger. He decides that he must return home, and the words he plans to say are significant. He recognizes that what he has done is first an offence against God himself ('I have sinned against heaven ...') and then against his father ('... and before you'). He is no longer worthy of the honour attached to the name of 'son'. However, he is desperate: if he can be but a hired servant for his father, he will survive! That is the position he plans to seek.

It is interesting that he plans to return to his family home. One might think this a slightly unrealistic note for Jesus to put in. After the dislocation and shame he has caused, would he not have been reluctant to do this? Could he not have gone elsewhere in his own country, where there was plenty, and started afresh in a situation where his past was not known? That this was not his plan suggests, perhaps, that, in addition to the pangs of hunger, there was a yearning for his own family so strong that it drove out the fear of punishment or ostracism. News would have travelled fast in a village culture, between as well as within communities. Even in other parts of his Jewish homeland his behaviour as a rebellious son, a wastrel, one defiled by his dissolute living and contact with Gentiles, might well have become known. The strategy of returning to his own family was risky, but maybe he reckoned that it was, in fact, his own father who held his best hope for the future. It was his father whom he had wounded most deeply, but it was his father with whom, still, the bond was strongest.

He set off for home. In narrating this stage – 'he went to his father' – Jesus highlights the personal impetus again. Restored (though different) relationship is the goal, not just food. But here we reach the heart-stopping moment as attention suddenly shifts to the father himself. Before the listeners can dwell on the question of what reaction the son will get, the father appears. He has seen his son from afar and does not wait for him to reach the farm gates. Recognizing not only his son but his son's condition, no doubt guessing much if not all of what has been going on, he is overcome with love and longing. He throws traditional dignity to the winds and runs to meet him. Risking the hostility of the whole community, his embrace and kiss silently but eloquently speak the words his son never dared to anticipate.

The son starts to deliver his prepared speech, and, as is always observed, he is not able to finish it. He stops before the planned request to be a hired servant. Whether we are meant to envisage him already overcome by his father's forgiveness, and realizing, however incoherently, the inappropriateness of the planned request, or whether his father simply interrupts him, or whether the storyteller himself wanted to hasten on to the climax, we do not know, and it does not really matter. The father's response is given not directly to the son but in his orders to his slaves. These orders are a graphic instance of the power of words to bring about a whole new state of affairs. The robe is no mere covering for one who has lost all. The ring is no mere item of jewellery. The sandals are no mere protection for the feet. The calf is no mere food for the hungry. Each is a pregnant sign that, in intention and in fact, the young man is being restored to the status of son. For this is the 'best' robe, the father's own; the ring carries the family seal; the shoes signify freedom as opposed to slavery; the fatted calf means a great celebration for the whole village. Moreover, from the father's point of view, 'restoration' may be the wrong concept. 'This son of mine was dead and is alive again; he was lost, and is found.' He may have been disobedient and rebellious, but in the father's eyes, he had never ceased to be a son, and this treatment was the clearest possible way of showing it to him, and to everyone. Celebration was in order because he had been dead and lost: dead with regard to communal ties and ancestral faith; as good as dead physically; lost to his loved ones. Now he was alive again, in all senses, and found. Apparently without loss of time the partying begins.

The listeners have already experienced one remarkable and startling climax to the story in hearing of the father's welcome. But there is another twist to come. Suddenly the mood quietens. The feasting had begun, but out in the field, still, was the elder brother, supervising some of the hired hands, maybe, in the harvesting. As he approaches the house the sounds of music and dancing reach his ears and he asks a servant what is going on. Hearing what has happened, his response is not joy but anger. He will not join in the celebration.

Then his father appears. Just as he had gone out to meet his returning younger son, so he goes out to his loyal but reluctant elder one. His father beseeches him: neither the celebration, nor the unity and security of the family, will be complete without him. The elder brother, however, stakes out his position. He has been a loyal servant of his father for years, never breaking a rule. He feels hard done by because his father has never so much as given him a young goat so that he could have a party with his friends. But for his brother, who has flouted the most basic and serious of the commandments, and (in the elder's graphic phrase) 'eaten up your fortune with prostitutes', the father has laid on a top-class feast. It is hard not to feel the force of the elder brother's words.

Equally, it is hard now not to feel with the father, as he
has the final word in the story. The elder son is not right to
feel deprived, for he too now had his inheritance: all that
was the father's was his! *De facto*, he had reached the point
of maturity and equality with his father, but sadly it seems
he had neither realized it nor lived accordingly. And the
return of the younger son to the fold was an occasion worth
celebrating, whatever may have been the relationship of the
father to the elder, for it marked no less than a return from
death to life. The wholeness of the family unit, which had
been violated, had begun to be healed. They now awaited
only the elder brother's wholehearted entry to the celebration, and complete unity would be restored. But would he
come in? That is the question left hanging by Jesus.

We can imagine how this moving story would have drawn
Jesus' hearers into the scenes that it pictured, for he was not
talking about a strange and distant world, but about one
that was very familiar to them – a world of families, of love
and rebellion, of money and farming, of recklessness and
loyalty. And the events he recounted required a response.
What would his hearers have thought about the callous and
selfish departure of the younger son? Of the astonishing
forgiveness of the father? Of the stand-offish attitude of
the elder son? It is very unlikely that anyone who was really
listening could have remained neutral. For some, indeed,
the response would surely have gone deeper than just
taking up a stance of sympathy or hostility to one or other
of the characters. It would have entailed *identifying* with
them: saying 'that is me'. And in that identification the
story might have brought profound joy or sadness, yearning or remorse.

The setting in which Luke places the story is very plausible and helps us to imagine some of its potential impact
on different groups of people. Pharisees and Scribes have

been expressing disapproval of Jesus on account of his easy mixing with groups of people considered unclean – the customs officers and 'sinners' (Luke 15:1–2). Along with the pictures of a shepherd searching for his sheep and a woman searching for a lost coin, Jesus tells this story to these leading figures. But others too would be listening in, especially the 'sinners' themselves and Jesus' disciples.

Jesus invites his hearers to envisage a rebellious son who puts himself outside the pale of family, community and ancestral faith; who flouts God's law and ends up in the most shameful state of uncleanness – in the household of a Gentile, feeding pigs. What would they think of him? For the Pharisees and Scribes, such a person would be the very personification of a reprobate, someone whose company a strict law-abiding Jew would shun. Little sympathy for the son would come from that quarter. The customs officers, prostitutes and others labelled 'sinners', however, although they might have agreed with the Pharisees and Scribes in mentally disapproving of the son's actions, would very likely have found some fellow feeling with him. They would have understood, perhaps, the motives of desperation that led him to demand his fortune and seek control of his own destiny. In times of economic upheaval, these would have been very similar motives to those that drove the 'sinners' themselves into the pay of Gentile Romans, or of other Jews who had lapsed into immoral ways, perhaps as pimps. Similarly, different members of the audience would have reacted differently to the son's decision to return; the Pharisees and Scribes looking cynically at his motives; the customs officers and 'sinners' recognizing a familiar pattern of desperation.

How then would both groups have reacted on hearing of the father's unexpected and overwhelming welcome when his good-for-nothing son returned? Here Jesus gives us one of the most exquisite and enduring pictures of the possibility of love; but we must not, on account of its familiarity, reduce it to mere doctrinal statement or moral exhortation. Jesus says neither 'this is what God is like' nor 'this is what you must be like'. He simply paints the picture. With vivid strokes – the sight 'afar off', the running, the embracing, the robe, ring, shoes and calf – he shows a man caught up in the movement of compassion and reconciliation. He has no need to say 'this is the right way'. The picture itself says all that needs to be said and more, and, in its eloquence, almost compels a reaction.

What might the Pharisees listening to Jesus have thought? Initially, perhaps, there was shock and disapproval, but then maybe, for some, a gradually dawning sense of a new possibility: that *they could themselves take up the position of the father in the story* with respect to the 'sinners' they had hitherto so despised. How can we encapsulate the feelings of such hearers, being opened up to a startlingly new vision? For those who allowed themselves to be moved beyond their first disdain for this feckless youth, to identify with the feelings of his father, it would have been a deeply unsettling time as the prejudices and fixed mindset of years started to crumble and their world began to be reshaped. Perhaps the first stirrings of an undreamed-of hope were there too, but we should not underestimate the sense of dislocation and disturbance, which would have surely have been the first response of any who did not immediately close their ears to the story. Some, with numbing shock, might have started to see that they had more in common with the prodigal himself than they could ever have imagined. And the 'sinners'? They had already had a taste of a different kind of society, via this teacher who was obviously devoted to God and his requirements, and yet was happy to eat and drink with them. The story would simply have reinforced and sweetened that taste, as it portrayed, in the figure of the father, unlooked-for acceptance of the outcast.

Then comes the moment when the spotlight turns on the elder brother. One can almost hear the thud of sudden recognition as the identification is made by Jesus' hearers between this brother and the law-abiding critics of Jesus. Equally, one can almost see the walls of defence being erected by those for whom the story was proving just too unsettling. Yet neither Pharisees nor 'sinners' would be allowed to feel that Jesus was merely poking fun at the guardians of the law. The father in his story loves both sons. He affirms that the elder is 'always with him'; they share ownership of everything. He longs for him to join in the celebrations of his brother's return. And at the end of the story the hearers are wondering whether he will in fact do so. It is a poignantly inviting ending. It poses the implicit question to the critics: will *you* drop your guard and start to party? And it gently warns the 'sinners': don't let the attentions of this fun-loving teacher lead you to reject your brothers the Pharisees and Scribes, even though they have rejected you.

All the while the disciples, too, would have been listening, and perhaps watching the faces of the other listeners. Slowly they were learning from Jesus. For them too this story would have been pregnant with suggestion. In the harsh life of first-century Palestine what options for living were open to them? One way might seem to be that of cutting loose from law and custom, and finding what pleasure they could, whether in pagan surroundings or not. Another option might be to fly the flag ever higher for the ancient traditions of the homeland, which meant (like the Pharisees) taking a rigid line towards those who seemed to compromise. But a third way, revealed through story's gentle art of unveiling fresh possibilities, was that of a father striving to reconcile his children: a father for whom people were more important than property; unity more important than dignity; forgiveness more important than family honour; reconciliation more important than national and ritual purity. Into such a way they were already being drawn by the teller of the tale, and the tale could have given them a fresh glimpse into the meaning of what he was doing.

9

Looming Unemployment

The Shrewd Manager:
Luke 16:1–9

Then Jesus said to the disciples, 'There was a rich man who had a manager, and charges were brought to him that this man was squandering his property. So he summoned him and said to him, "What is this that I hear about you? Give me an accounting of your management, because you cannot be my manager any longer." Then the manager said to himself, "What will I do, now that my master is taking the position away from me? I am not strong enough to dig, and I am ashamed to beg. I have decided what to do so that, when I am dismissed as manager, people may welcome me into their homes." So, summoning his master's debtors one by one, he asked the first, "How much do you owe my master?" He answered, "A hundred jugs of olive oil." He said to him, "Take your bill, sit down quickly, and make it fifty." Then he asked another, "And how much do you owe?" He replied, "A hundred containers of wheat." He said to him, "Take your bill and make it eighty." And his master commended the dishonest manager because he had acted shrewdly; for the children of this age are more shrewd in dealing with their own generation than are the children of light. And I tell you, make friends for yourselves by means of dishonest wealth so that when it is gone, they may welcome you into the eternal homes.'

This seems a strange story. People down the centuries have agreed. How could a person with so great a moral authority as Jesus have given his blessing to such underhand tactics to secure one's future, as he appears to do here? Many answers have been proposed to the puzzle. Here we concentrate on one reading of the story that seems to make sense. As with the other parables, the most important clue lies in envisaging the actual social situation that the story pictures.

For the wealthy landowners of Palestine (and elsewhere in the Roman Empire) a 'manager' or 'steward' was a vital subordinate. He was an official in charge of collecting the rent due from tenants – small farmers – and dealing with other financial transactions such as the sale of grain and other produce. He exercised considerable authority over the landowner's affairs.

Such officials, however, were vulnerable as well as vital. They were certainly better off than the tenants they dealt with, but remained far below the landowners in both wealth and power. Though it was probably common practice for managers to increase rents and charges, to allow them to make a profit for themselves on the various transactions, it did not do to allow this to become too noticeable. This was due not so much to any love of upright dealings on the part of the employers as to an acute sense of social hierarchy. The subordinate could not be allowed to appear as lavish in lifestyle as the superior. If he did, the suspicion would always be aroused that he was not only profiting from the dealings he engaged in on his employer's behalf, but also depriving the employer of some of his rightful revenue. Such suspicions could, in the case of a harsh employer, lead to swift dismissal, and there were no tribunals to appeal to.

Plenty of ambitious men would be waiting in the wings to fill the vacant post.

This, however, was only one side of the manager's vulnerability. If the tenants or merchants with whom he did business resented his attitude or his tactics of self-enrichment one of the few things they could safely do about it was bring tales of his behaviour to the employer. These clients, too, had their daily needs. Many were very poor. Polite negotiation would often have seemed far from adequate in situations of urgency and despair. As in big and small business in many parts of the world today there was a harsh, cut-throat atmosphere. Managers with superiors must watch their backs.

This background lies behind the scene conjured up by Jesus for his hearers: 'There was a rich man who had a manager, and charges were brought to him that this man was squandering his property.' Aware of the background, we are alert to the normal expectations of standard characters. The 'rich man' would have been assumed to be one of the remote élite, fantastically wealthy in the eyes of the majority, wielding enormous power over them and sullenly resented or secretly envied. The manager would have been assumed to be a worldly-wise character who had thus far been able to retain the favour of both employer and clients. The accusers would have been one or more groups of clients and their accusations may have contained more or less truth. The charge that the manager was 'squandering' the rich man's property has an immediate resonance with the preceding story in which the younger son 'squanders' his share of the family inheritance. This was the charge precisely calculated to bring about the manager's downfall: a luxurious lifestyle, which transgressed the boundaries of his station, raised the suspicion that he was creaming off more of his master's revenues than he ought.

So it is not a black and white moral world into which the
story invites us, with heroes and villains readily identifiable
as such. It is the same morally ambiguous world with
which we are so familiar in our own time. This is one of the
peculiar aspects of fascination in these tales of Jesus, and
this one in particular.

The employer acts quite predictably: he sacks the
manager on the spot, simply telling him to bring back the
account book (the meaning of 'give me an accounting of
your management'). At this point, however, the steward's
cunning comes into play. Luke allows us to overhear the
deliberations going on inside his head (like those of several
other characters in parables he recounts). We see the real
desperation of his position. When he says that he is not
strong enough to dig and is ashamed to beg we should not
imagine that he is merely being feeble minded. We are given
an insight here into the bleak range of options that might in
fact have been available to him. Sacked as a manager, he
could not hope to get another similar post. Presumably
he had long since left the family home. Apparently he had
no 'transferable skills' that might get him employment as an
artisan of some kind. He might get work as a day-labourer
('digging'), but after years of earning his living in management he would not be able to cope for long with manual
labour. After that, what was there? With no 'social security'
there was one option only: beggary. It is revealing and
poignant that he says he would be *ashamed* to beg. Then, as
now, the utter humiliation of descent from an accepted
place in society – however humble – to begging for survival
would have been the most powerful of incentives to do
everything possible to avoid it.

The manager, therefore, saw only one goal to aim for: to
be 'welcomed into people's homes'. What does that mean?
That he would put people so much in his debt that, as a
result of their eternal gratitude, he would be able to go

round from one client's house to another's, enjoying their hospitality to the end of his days? This seems an unlikely goal – little better than the beggary of which he would be so ashamed. It is much more probable that the 'homes' he was thinking of were the great 'households' of the rich – like the one in which he had up to now been serving – and that what he had in mind was the possibility of another job. It was as a manager that he had kept body and soul together thus far, and it was as a manager that he meant to continue.

So he makes his plan and executes it. We need to remember that the clients he summons would not yet know that he had been sacked. As far as they were concerned he was still acting with the full authority of his employer. The clients here were probably merchants who had received some of the rich man's produce to sell, and owed him the proceeds, plus interest. The amount of debt is here stated in terms of quantity of produce, but would be repaid, of course, in money. To charge such interest was common practice, but was against the Jewish law. This was not a piece of petty legalism, but a law designed to prevent the rich getting inordinately richer at the expense of the poor. It seems likely that the amount by which the manager reduces the clients' debts was the amount of interest normally charged on these products.

How, though, would this strategy help the manager achieve his goal of becoming employable again? It might appear as though it would do little more than win him some short-term popularity with the clients. The game would soon be up; the employer would find out; still worse punishment would come upon the manager; and the clients would be required to pay up anyway under the new regime. This, however, is to reckon without the powerful social forces operating in the culture, compelling people to recognize the importance of being held in honour in the community's eyes.

What the manager has done, albeit without his ex-employer's authority, is make the rich man newly popular in the eyes of his clients. They think, for a short while at least, that he has suddenly started showing a new streak of compassion and a new attentiveness to the law. But, once the truth comes out, the employer is in no mind to reverse the manager's unilateral act. It will do him no good to forfeit his newly found position of esteem. More important still for the manager, the landowner recognizes the skill and shrewdness of his subordinate's action. One can almost see a wry smile cross his lips as the jealousy and ruthlessness that led him to dismiss the manager turn to admiration, indeed gratitude. 'And his master commended the dishonest manager because he had acted shrewdly.' The manager has done even more than display to all and sundry how employable he remains; it looks very much as if he has succeeded in getting his old job back.

Why might Jesus have told a tale like this? Like the story of the lost but returning son preceding it, it would have given his hearers a surprising but hopeful glimpse of a desperate situation reversed, of relationships put on a new footing. It is, like the other tales, very much a story of the everyday world. None of these figures are held up as spotless ideals. But the manager's actions suggest the possibility of wise and indeed just action in the very midst of the mundane murkiness of hard financial dealings. The 'shrewdness' for which he is commended by his employer (and, implicitly, by Jesus himself) is surely more than the possession of a cool head in a crisis. It carries with it the associations of the Jewish ideal of wisdom – a concept and a quality which held together both common-sense prudence and obedience to God's law. In his cancelling of interest he was pursuing his own agenda, but he was also doing what was right – indeed, he was showing his employer the way – and the employer's recognition of his wisdom shows that he, too, was perhaps starting to see things differently.

The manager is called 'unrighteous', then, not because his emergency measures were crooked or deceitful, but because – like the tax collectors – he was seen as involved in a tainted occupation, working for the alien landowner (maybe a Roman, at least a collaborator), dependent for his livelihood on 'dirty money'. But like the lost and found son, who went and fed a Gentile's pigs, the story leaves this man in the light of acceptance and favour. A postscript by the narrator comments that 'the children of this age are more shrewd in dealing with their own generation than are the children of light'. Those who regarded themselves as 'children of light' would have despised a 'child of this age', such as the manager, but he shows himself truly wise – both prudent and just.

The concluding application of the story is – fittingly – as puzzling at first sight as the story itself. Could Jesus really have advised people to buy favour with others 'with dishonest wealth'? And – worse still! – could he really have suggested that such tactics would win an eternal reward? But our explanation of the story should make this application more comprehensible too. The 'wealth' Jesus is speaking about is 'dishonest' or 'unrighteous' in just the sense that the manager himself is. He is caught up in a system perceived by the pious as tainted, but a system that is an inescapable part of most people's lives. The money that we handle can be used meanly or generously, crookedly or justly. The consequence of a generous and just use of money, such as the manager engaged in as his self-rescue package, is new friendship, true relationship, on a much more subtle and significant level than the mere buying of favours by bribery. Those who heard Jesus would not all be estate managers, but they could all aspire to acceptance in 'eternal tabernacles', 'homes of the new age'. This phrase, exactly like the picture of the welcoming home discovered by the lost son, suggests both a human and a divine reception for the wise followers of Jesus. Money itself will not last; it will 'fail'. But those who use it generously and justly are assured of a future of human friendship and divine blessing.

10

Enforced Separation

The Rich Man and Lazarus:
Luke 16:19–31

'There was a rich man who was dressed in purple and fine linen and who feasted sumptuously every day. And at his gate lay a poor man named Lazarus, covered with sores, who longed to satisfy his hunger with what fell from the rich man's table; even the dogs would come and lick his sores. The poor man died and was carried away by the angels to be with Abraham. The rich man also died and was buried. In Hades, where he was being tormented, he looked up and saw Abraham far away with Lazarus by his side. He called out, "Father Abraham, have mercy on me, and send Lazarus to dip the tip of his finger in water and cool my tongue; for I am in agony in these flames." But Abraham said, "Child, remember that during your lifetime you received your good things, and Lazarus in like manner evil things; but now he is comforted here, and you are in agony. Besides all this, between you and us a great chasm has been fixed, so that those who might want to pass from here to you cannot do so, and no one can cross from there to us." He said, "Then, father, I beg you to send him to my father's house – for I have five brothers – that he may warn them, so that they will not also come into this place of torment." Abraham replied, "They have Moses and the prophets; they should listen to them." He said, "No, father Abraham; but if someone goes to them from the dead, they will repent." He said to him, "If they do not listen to Moses and the prophets, neither will they be convinced even if someone rises from the dead." '

Between the richest and the poorest there lay, in Jesus' day as in ours, an enormous gulf. It was a gulf not only of possessions but of experience and of social standing. The beginning of this tale pictures for us the stark contrast, not by marshalling statistics or bland generalities, but by introducing us to two individual human beings. They lived, in fact, cheek by jowl – just as today one can drive through the suburbs of a city and pass very suddenly from an area of affluence to an area of deprivation. But in every way other than the geographical, they were poles apart. Tragically, it was a distance that was to endure beyond death.

The rich man could be clearly identified as such by his dress and his lifestyle. In the ancient world, as in the modern, much of the purpose of accumulating wealth was conspicuous display – being *seen* to be wealthy. He had money to buy expensive cloth from abroad. He feasted lavishly, not just when there was a special occasion to celebrate (like a wayward son returning home), but *every day*. This man was undoubtedly one of those whom the sociologists call the 'élite' – the tiny minority at the top of the social pinnacle. Such people were the landowners, Romans or Jewish friends of the Romans, who had gradually accumulated more and more of the land of the poor. This man appears to have been a Jew, for we learn later that his brothers (and presumably he himself) could be expected to be familiar with 'Moses and the prophets'.

The poor man is unusual in Jesus' tales: he has a name. Lazarus means 'the one whom God helps', which is doubtless significant. No one else appears to be giving him any effective help apart from 'laying' him at the rich man's gate.

The passive expression here implies that he had become too weak to take himself there: someone, at least, had had enough pity on him to take him to a place where he might receive some charity. Lazarus was no doubt one of those driven off the land on account of its increasing devolvement into the hands of a few. Deprived of the support of family, of loved ones to sustain his life, his body was disfigured with sores on the outside and empty with hunger inside. The words 'longed to satisfy his hunger' are exactly the same as those used of the prodigal son in the famine. Just as the prodigal longed – but failed – to satisfy himself with the carob pods meant for the pigs, so this poor man longed – but failed – to satisfy himself with the meagre scraps that were brought to him (as a sop to conscience or with genuine good intention by some servant or other) from the rich man's fine meals. The seal would have been set on his degradation by the pariah dogs, which came to lick his cracked and diseased skin.

Here was a scene probably familiar to Jesus' hearers. It would have appeared to many pious eyes as if God, far from helping Lazarus, had completely abandoned him. His name would have sounded sadly ironic. The rich man, by contrast, would have been thought by many to be blessed by God. How else could one explain the acute difference between the conditions of the two men?

Without narrating any specific action by either man, Jesus says that they both died. This is the turning point, for death comes with equal and unnerving regularity to rich as to poor, uniting and levelling all. Lazarus dies first: people in his condition, physical and social, could not expect to survive for long. He was carried by the angels into Abraham's bosom (according to common piety the place of care and security for those blessed by God). This surely comes as a jolt to the received wisdom that, being in an unfortunate condition means that God is against you. But then the rich man dies, and, pointedly, he *was buried*. Lazarus would have received no such formality, but was perhaps just dragged away to a refuse tip. These obsequies, however, were to be the last piece of pampering for the rich man, for he receives no angelic escort to a safe haven. Abruptly we see him in Hades, the place of torture. Unity in death was not to endure. It is as if the two men's paths have crossed, briefly, at last, but then continue in a straight line, away from one another, and end up as far apart as before.

At this solemn, terrible moment, the rich man looks up and *sees*. We have thus far received no indication that he had ever been truly aware of Lazarus. It is interesting to note that in the Bible compassion is preceded by *seeing*. God *saw* the plight of his people in Egypt and came to rescue them (Exodus 2:25; 3:7–8). The Samaritan *saw* the plight of the wounded man, had compassion, and came to bind up his wounds. But only now does the rich man *see* Lazarus, when it is too late to help him, when it is fully evident that God (alone) has indeed helped him in the end. God has lived up to his name of being the one who raises the poor from the ash-heap (Psalm 113:7). Now it is the rich man who needs help, and he is bold enough to ask for it.

It seems that even in his torment he still regards Lazarus as a lesser mortal, someone to be sent on errands. He cries out to Abraham to send Lazarus to ease his torture by dipping his finger in water and cooling his burning tongue. Probably he thinks he has an ally in Abraham: the patriarch of the Jewish race had been famously wealthy, and therefore to the rich man was 'one of us'. He had perhaps forgotten that Abraham was also held up in tradition as a model of hospitality.

There is a sad and sombre tone to Abraham's reply. His addressing the rich man familiarly as 'son', 'child' – just as the father had addressed the elder brother in the parable of

The Prodigal Son – is a way of acknowledging that this rich man, just like his poor neighbour, is still a child of the covenant, a member of God's family, a 'child of Abraham' like Zacchaeus the chief customs officer (Luke 19:9) or the crippled woman Jesus healed on the Sabbath (Luke 13:6). Abraham's message is simple. He tells the rich man to remember that in his lifetime he had enjoyed good things, while Lazarus had suffered evil things, and he points to the fact that now the positions are reversed. Lazarus is in the place of comfort; the rich man is in the place of anguish. The point is understated, but fearfully lucid. Justice is now being done.

Abraham then adds that there is a great gulf now fixed between the place of safety and the place of torment. It would be simply impossible for Lazarus, or anyone else, to respond to pleas for help such as the rich man has just uttered. And it would be equally impossible for those in the place of torment to escape to the other side.

The rich man (or rather the 'once-rich man') is not giving up. He still has the notion of Lazarus as an errand boy in mind. In desperation, he pleads that Lazarus be sent to his father's house, to warn his five brothers still living at home. This request would turn out to be as fruitless as the first, but it is interesting that in it we see at last a glimmer of altruism as well as a telling admission of what he now knows: that his torment is not unjust, but is a direct consequence of the way that he had lived. There might, he feels, be hope for others living as he had done if they could but see how their behaviour would be punished.

The response from Abraham is brief. 'They have Moses and the prophets; let them hear them.' The brothers knew the will of God, his commands, his promises of blessing to those who kept the covenant, his warnings to the disobedient, as written in their Scriptures, faithfully handed down through the centuries. Those commands included, of course, that of caring for the poor. What more did they need?

The man has one last try. Surely, if someone comes back from the dead to warn them, they will repent? But Abraham knows that is not the way human nature works. People are not stunned by strange happenings into changing the orientation of their lives. No, is his laconic reply – one imagines a sad, slow shake of the head. No, if they do not listen to Moses and the prophets, not even a resurrection will convince them to mend their ways. And here the story ends.

As with his other stories, Jesus has not so much laid out a doctrine as invited his hearers to imagine a scene. This one is a simple scene, in two stages. First, a familiar picture from everyday life: two characters, one rich, the other poor, so close, yet so far away. Second, a 'behind-the-scenes' look at what happened after their deaths. This second stage would have been a shocking one because most hearers would automatically have assumed that wealth was a sign of God's blessing. In a needling way, Jesus suggests that the standard expectation needs to be turned on its head.

It is important to realize that the aim of the story is not to give some sort of geographical information about the afterlife. In drawing the picture of Abraham's bosom, the torments of Hades, and the great gulf between, Jesus is using standard Jewish images of the time. Like all such images they are attempts to picture what cannot be pictured. But the painful clarity of the two alternatives – safety or torture – cannot be avoided.

It is of great interest to note the stress here on the meaning of death's finality. A person's way of life, it is implied, determines decisively what happens to them after death. Furthermore, that fate is not reversible. And only beyond death is direct knowledge of the fate of the wicked possible.

Such knowledge is denied to those still living, who have enough light by which to lead their lives.

But the burning question that we, like – no doubt – many of those who first heard the story, are left pondering is surely this: what was the sin of the rich man and his brothers? Recognizing correctly that in the Bible possession of riches is not itself regarded as sinful, some readers have assumed that these people must have been wicked in some way not mentioned at all in the story. Perhaps, it is said, they were adulterers or murderers. Similarly, recognizing that poverty is not in itself a virtue, people have ascribed to Lazarus humility, or patience, or obedience – something that seems to prepare him for his destination in the bosom of Abraham.

The problem with such an interpretation, however, is that it ignores the one key contrast that the story *does* explicitly draw between the two men: one was rich, the other poor. Somehow their fate must be related to that picture of abject misery before a house of opulence and feasting. Surely it is precisely the fact that the rich man never allowed himself to notice Lazarus on which we are to focus; that the crumbs from the rich man's table were not enough even for the poor man's survival, let alone for a dignified life in society. The sin was that of sheer neglect, of imagining that one could just get richer without any sense of responsibility for the use of one's wealth, or the welfare of the poor. Conversely, Jesus surely didn't want to make an issue of Lazarus's moral stance. The picture of the sick beggar, lifted at last by special messengers to a family home, is the picture of one whom God has indeed helped in the end, not of one who has *done* anything particularly praiseworthy. What, especially in his latter years, has Lazarus been *able* to do? It is a glimpse of *God's* kingdom come.

And so this story, which addresses so clearly the issue of individual responsibility and peers behind the curtain to the matter of individual destiny in a way unique among Jesus' stories, opens out equally clearly, like the other tales, on to the social world. Ultimately the story makes us think not simply of what will happen to us (or others) when we die, but of the total unacceptability, in God's eyes, of a world where extravagance can co-exist beside slow, grinding deaths from penury and disease. It invites us not to give up bothering about this world because we are waiting for a better, but to start bothering about it, for this is our only chance to do so. It holds out no easy hope of instant transformation, no false promise that God always leads people to safety and peace *before* death. But it pulls no punches in its picture of retribution for the wicked, identified by the colours of callous neglect. And at the same time it vividly evokes a future in which there is abundant compensation for years of injustice suffered and the tears of the poor are wiped away.

11

Godless Officialdom

The Judge and the Widow:
Luke 18:1–8

Then Jesus told them a parable about their need to pray always and not to lose heart. He said, 'In a certain city there was a judge who neither feared God nor had respect for people. In that city there was a widow who kept coming to him and saying, "Grant me justice against my opponent." For a while he refused; but later he said to himself, "Though I have no fear of God and no respect for anyone, yet because this widow keeps bothering me, I will grant her justice, so that she may not wear me out by continually coming." And the Lord said, "Listen to what the unjust judge says. And will not God grant justice to his chosen ones who cry to him day and night? Will he delay long in helping them? I tell you, he will quickly grant justice to them. And yet, when the Son of Man comes, will he find faith on earth?"'

Here is another tale in which two graphically contrasting individuals are introduced to us. Jesus paints them with quick, spare brushstrokes, quite sufficient for his hearers to envisage the kind of live characters they knew so well. Luke tells us that Jesus told the story as an encouragement to

pray, but we shall have to wait until we have thought about
the story until we can see how it works in this way.

First there is a judge. This official was clearly not a pious
Jew. He may have been someone of mixed stock, or a
Roman, or a Jew who collaborated with the Roman authorities, like the customs or tax officers that we meet a number
of times in the Gospel stories. Whatever his background,
he 'neither feared God nor had respect for people'. It is
possible that *he* might have considered the latter quality –
having no respect for people – as a virtue in his job; he might
have thought of it as 'impartiality'. However, the former
quality – not fearing God – is unequivocally negative in
biblical terms. In the Hebrew Scriptures the 'fear of God',
an attitude of profound reverence before him, is seen as the
beginning of wisdom. It is the attitude from which springs a
careful obedience to God's commands, and one of the prime
commands, emanating from the very character of God,
was to see that justice was done for the most vulnerable in
society, typically represented by the widow and the orphan.
Such 'justice' or 'righteousness' was not a matter of mere
cool 'impartiality', but of striving to see that life and dignity
were preserved for those most at risk of losing them. God's
'righteousness' was an active, not a passive, concept – he
acted to save those the world left to one side and allowed to
go to the wall. His people, and not least their leaders, were
to imitate him.

So, when the next character is introduced, a widow, the
hearers do not expect her to get a hearing from this particular judge. Widows were in an extremely exposed position
socially in the Palestinian culture of Jesus' day, as in many
societies before and since. With no state aid, pensions or
benefits, they were dependent financially on the support of
such family members who were left and willing to give it.
They were, of course, often young. In a society where
the honour of women was closely bound up with that of

their menfolk – husbands, fathers, sons, brothers – a widow left on her own was likely to be in a position not only of insecurity but also of shame. But immediately this widow is seen in a surprising light. She is not weak and passive. She appears in public, coming frequently to the judge, seeking redress against an 'opponent'.

The situation presupposed here is a fairly rudimentary system of 'justice' in which the power of decision was concentrated entirely in the judge's hands. There was no court system, no jury, no prosecution and defence counsel, no system of checks and balances, no appeal tribunal. And this was clearly a desperate woman, that she would expose herself to public shame in this way, coming personally to badger the judge. He was her only hope. Who the 'opponent' was, or what the dispute was over, we are not told – very likely we are to imagine some argument over property. Some ruthless person had perhaps laid claim to the widow's little plot of land, and a judicial ruling was her only chance of a good outcome.

To begin with, the judge tries to ignore her. True to his character of 'not respecting people' he is unmoved by the widow's pleadings. Perhaps we are to envisage him rationalizing this to himself as impartiality ('don't be swayed by emotion'); but from the outside it looks very like sheer callousness. Then, however, he starts to give way. In an internal dialogue, like that of the estate manager, we overhear his reasoning. Starting by bolstering his own sense of the kind of man he is ('Though I have no fear of God and no respect for anyone': we could translate this psychologically as 'It's all right, I'm not weakening') he decides to give in simply for the sake of a quiet life. The widow is being such a nuisance. He can see himself getting 'worn out' by her endless visits. The meaning may be even stronger: the word for 'wear out' literally means 'give a black eye'. No doubt he wasn't really afraid of serious physical harm, but he wanted to avoid any embarrassing bother from this persistent, desperate woman.

Here, with typical abruptness, the story itself ends. There is not even a word to indicate that the judge did what he had decided to do, let alone anything about the widow's reaction. The following verses contain Jesus' comments on the story.

The first comment calls the hearers especially to ponder 'what the unrighteous judge says'. The judge, it is quite clear, is a man of the world for whom the compassionate righteousness of the God of Israel is an alien thing. His giving in to the widow's request owes nothing to any high principle or sudden conversion. He is just fed up with being nagged. *And yet* we are led to assume at the end of the story that the widow got the justice she was seeking. It is a story of hope: even under the hostile rule of godless, amoral leaders, God's will may be done, his kingdom come.

Jesus then goes on to speak directly of God. The story of the judge and the widow opens out on to the great story of God and his suffering people, his 'elect'. God will indeed reach out in saving righteousness to his children who cry to him. Surely *he* will not delay long, as if one had to nag him until, eventually, he grudgingly gave in!

There is a puzzle here that is not resolved unless we clearly focus on the dynamics of the story. We naturally make some sort of link between the judge in the story and God, and the words of Jesus following the story seem to confirm that. It is a 'how much more' link: if even a crotchety old Roman judge eventually acts justly, despite himself, can we not have infinitely more confidence in the gracious God of Israel? But things are not quite as simple as this. The very reason Jesus told the parable, Luke says, was so that people would *keep praying* and not lose heart.

This presupposes a situation in which *it often really seems as if God is as reluctant as the judge in the story*!

How, then, can the story be an encouragement to pray? On the one hand, Jesus can surely not be saying that God is *like* a godless human judge – and even if he were saying that, it would hardly give his hearers much heart! On the other hand, if Jesus is simply emphasizing the *contrast* between God and the judge, why tell the story at all, if it gives no incentive to pray by emphasizing the character of God?

The solution seems to be this. In the story of the judge and the widow, Jesus is pointing – as in many other parables – to a surprising and hopeful sign of God's kingdom. He is asking his hearers to discern the possibility that even in the worldly-wise ruminations of a weary human judge *God* was bringing about his justice. The Old Testament writers believed that when human beings, including especially their rulers, did what was just and wise, God himself was at work through them. And real justice could be done even when motives were decidedly mixed. In the modern world we have a tendency to focus on the internal aspects of moral decisions. But for the widow in the story – like many others in her position, in real life then and now – the motivations of the judge are completely irrelevant. What matters is that he makes a decision that enables her to keep her little house, or whatever it was that her 'opponent' was unjustly claiming from her. Justice is concrete and practical. The issue in the story, then, is not whether the judge is 'like' or 'unlike' God. What the hearers would have been invited to see and imagine as the story was told was a world where justice was done – and therefore God was at work – even though the holders of power neither feared God nor cared for people.

Jesus, then, is pointing to the fact that, even in the present, in the very unpropitious circumstances of Roman overlordship, there are visible signs of justice: God's kingdom is coming. Events such as this were happening – those with

eyes opened could see them. This is indeed an encouragement to his hearers to pray: they do not have to imagine an
unseen future when God would answer; he was answering
now. He was hearing the cries of widows to judges as if they
were cries to himself. In the self-serving deliberations of the
judges he was sovereignly at work to answer. This fits with
the new vision of the world Jesus seems to have been seeking
to open up for his hearers – a vision in which they did
not have to rebel against their foreign rulers or retreat into
isolation in order to see the longed-for rule of God. They
could see it in the messy, 'defiled' situation under alien lords
in which they were even now immersed.

But Jesus' final comment is a sober one. 'And yet, when
the Son of Man comes, will he find faith on earth?' The
'coming' of the 'Son of Man', spoken of in the book of
Daniel, chapter 7, was one picture for the ultimate victory
of God's people Israel over their enemies. In using the
phrase 'Son of Man' of himself Jesus signalled that he was
taking the destiny of Israel on to his own shoulders. He also
made it clear that the means and nature of the victory to
which he looked were very different from standard expectation: the Son of Man must suffer and die. And in this final
saying, following the story, Jesus muses whether even in the
very hour of his victory there will be faith – trust that God is
working his purposes out.

The fact that Jesus faces here is that, notwithstanding the
signs of God's kingdom, it remains largely veiled. It is often
a struggle even for people of faith to see it – how much more
those who are not disposed to trust in God at all! Patience
and perseverance are called for. The widow remains a
poignant picture of God's suffering people calling out to
him continually. They must do so, not because he is reluctant or slow, but because those who should be his agents
on earth, people in authority, are reluctant and slow;
because evil is abroad and the faith of God's people is the

only bulwark on earth against it. This calling out to God takes place not only in their secret cries to their heavenly Father, but also as they plead, shamelessly, with the human authorities who have it in their power to make significant alterations to the course of events and bring about concrete justice.

But let us return finally to the story, and the picture of a cold-hearted functionary doing justice for a desperate widow. Faith must often go without sight, but it is given from time to time little shafts of light, windows on to the possible and the real. These moments of insight keep it going. This is one such window, opened by Jesus to help the suffering faithful on their way.

12

Worshipping Apart

The Pharisee and the Tax Collector:
Luke 18:9–14

He also told this parable to some who trusted in themselves that they were righteous and regarded others with contempt: 'Two men went up to the temple to pray, one a Pharisee and the other a tax collector. The Pharisee, standing by himself, was praying thus, "God, I thank you that I am not like other people: thieves, rogues, adulterers, or even like this tax collector. I fast twice a week; I give a tenth of all my income." But the tax collector, standing far off, would not even look up to heaven, but was beating his breast and saying, "God, be merciful to me, a sinner!" I tell you, this man went down to his home justified rather than the other; for all who exalt themselves will be humbled, but all who humble themselves will be exalted.'

It seems to have been one of Jesus' main aims, not least in his parables, to undermine the self-confidence of those who were too sure of their acceptability to God and to raise the confidence of those who hardly dared to hope that God might accept them. This story, immediately following on in Luke from the one we considered in the previous chapter, is as pointed as any.

Like many of the other stories, it calls for imagination of a scene that begins in a familiar enough way, but ends with a surprising twist. The hearers are invited to think: could this really be so? Could a Samaritan help a wounded Jew? Could a godless judge do justice for a desperate widow? And here, could a tax collector turn out to be acceptable to God, rather than a pious Pharisee? Moreover, there is something in the very form of the stories that inspires hope (or, depending on the hearers, perhaps fear!) that the answer is yes. They are only stories – probably fictional ones – and even if any of them recount actual events, those events may be isolated and unusual. But in the very telling of them, the very naming of the possibility, Jesus gets under the skin of his hearers, subverts standard views, and subtly, even subliminally, makes an alternative outlook seem suddenly tenable.

This is the only one of Jesus' stories to be set in the Temple. Immediately the imposing building – still under construction in Jesus' day, following the destruction of its two predecessors – rises up in the mind's eye of his hearers. This was the sacred centre of a sacred city, which was itself the sacred centre of a sacred land. It was the focus for every Jew's devotion, and those who lived within reach could enter and pray. It would have been the custom for people to gather especially at the times of the twice-daily sacrifices. Luke 1:10 shows us Zacharias, father of John the Baptist, burning incense in the inner sanctum while a great crowd of worshippers stands outside. Male Jews could penetrate furthest towards the heart of the sanctuary. Women and Gentiles each had their courts further out.

The Scriptures had stressed the holiness of God's 'courts' and the need for those who drew near to God there to possess 'clean hands and a pure heart' (see especially Psalms 15 and 24). It would be of instant interest to Jesus' hearers, therefore, to hear about a Pharisee and a customs officer both going up to the Temple to pray. The Pharisees were a group who laid great stress on the correct observance of the law in every particular; who, indeed, were guardians of a tradition of interpretation of the law which sought to make it applicable for contemporary times, and therefore went into a good deal more detail than the law itself. They genuinely believed that this was the way God wanted his people to live at a time when their ancestral customs, and to some extent their very identity, were under threat. They believed that this path of detailed law observance – not the paths of political activism, or violent rebellion, or mere acquiescence in the status quo – was the way to be true Jews in their current situation and the way to hasten the coming of God's kingdom. Their insistence on this way no doubt made them unpopular with some, but certainly earned them respect, even among those who felt they could never aspire to such levels of devotion. It would therefore be no surprise to see a Pharisee dutifully entering the temple gates to go and pray; and it would have been taken for granted that his prayer would be acceptable to God.

The tax collector was different altogether. Bracketed with those labelled 'sinners' several times in the Gospels, tax collectors ('customs officers' may be a more accurate description, since the main taxation system was handled by the Romans themselves) were a generally despised class of people, Jews whose occupation in the pay of the Romans brought them both ritual impurity and unpopularity. They were among those who made no attempt to emulate the Pharisees and their like. Essentially, they had given up on the worthwhileness of serious obedience to the law.

One can understand some of the practical and economic reasons for this. Despite a fairly recent revival of Jewish nationalist fortunes under the Maccabees, a number of Jews must have seriously wondered, in the light of their recent history, how true it could be that obedience inevitably led to blessing and prosperity, as certain parts of their

Scriptures suggested. We have already seen the way in which ancestral land had been expropriated by the wealthy through extortionate rents and taxes. For many, sheer survival hung in the balance, and if an opportunity arose to make a decent living from the pagan rulers, one can imagine that they would jump at the chance, and never mind scruples about the law or associating with Gentiles. In effect, such collaborators were conniving in the enslavement of their fellow Jews, though without holding out any prospect of the seven-yearly release commanded in the law (Deuteronomy 15:12–18). In addition, their profession gave such people the opportunity to collect more than their dues, and increase their personal income (though also their unpopularity) further.

Yet such people, alienated as they were from mainstream Jewish piety, did not cease to have spiritual needs and longings. Their way of life surely arose, at least in part, from perplexity at the ways of God. They did not necessarily want to abandon the God of their ancestors. They did not set out perversely to cut themselves off from the community of faith. They could simply not be content with an attitude of pretence that all would be well if only one kept the law strictly enough. Perhaps they longed for the freedom to voice their perplexity; to air the doubts and questions posed by their history and their present.

And so we find a customs officer going to pray alongside the Pharisee. He is allowed in the Temple, apparently. But eyebrows would be raised at this pairing, and questions would start to be asked about whether the Owner of the Temple would really welcome this particular guest.

Now we observe and listen to the two worshippers in turn. As in several other stories Luke records for us what goes on unseen and unheard – except to God – in a person's heart. The Pharisee stands straight and gives thanks to God. The first cause for thanks is that he is not like other people.

This sounds unbearably snobbish to us, and indeed it is a part of the attitude that the story challenges, but it would not have been dismissed lightly by Jesus' hearers. We know of other ancient prayers of the rabbis in a similar vein. As we have seen, the Jewish people were in difficult straits. The Pharisaic response was one genuine, though in Jesus' eyes largely misguided, response to the situation. Keeping a strong hold on the sense of God's calling of a special people, and strictly observing the law as a way of marking out their identity and hastening the coming of God's kingdom, would have seemed one logical development from their ancient traditions. Nor should we overlook the fact that the Pharisee *thanks God* that he is not like other people: he recognizes fundamentally that the 'holiness' of Israel is God's gift.

Especially, he thanks God that he is not an 'extortioner', or 'unrighteous', an 'adulterer', or 'like this customs officer'. The words used here are suggestive of the kind of moral laxity that marked out the pagan rulers and those who consorted with them. The 'extortioners' he was thinking of could have been especially the rich foreigners who bought up the land and drove the native inhabitants into slavery, or their unscrupulous lackeys who did their dirty work for them and lined their own pockets in the process. In the latter category would have come the shrewd manager in Jesus' earlier story. He is called, significantly, 'unrighteous', which was almost certainly a word used to describe his type by the Pharisees. A more general word than 'extortioner', it has perhaps the connotation 'man of the world', someone who didn't go to great lengths to keep ritually clean by eating the right foods, avoiding contact with Gentiles and so on. Good Jews like the Pharisees would have been shocked by the incidence of 'adultery' in their land, with figures like King Herod leading the way in immoral practice (Mark 6:17–18). So, for this Pharisee, the tax collector standing nearby probably summed up all that he was thankful *not* to be: involved in dubious financial dealings; careless about purity laws; keeping Gentile company; and absorbing Gentile ways.

The Pharisee also mentions two of his own positive acts of piety, two of the main distinguishing marks of such people: fasting and tithing. He fasted twice a week, which was more even than the traditions current at the time required. Fasting was an outward sign of devotion signalling penitence for sin and the hope of God's mercy for oneself and the nation. He also gave tithes of *all* that he got, again exceeding the basic requirements, which stipulated that one give a tenth of grain, wine and oil only to the Temple treasury. In his own eyes, and the eyes of many of Jesus' hearers, this was an impressively holy man.

The customs officer's attitude in prayer presents a stark contrast to the Pharisee's. He stands 'far off' – at a safe distance either from the Pharisee or the inner court where the sacrifice was being offered, or both. His posture is telling: he does not raise his eyes heavenward, in confident manner, but beats his breast. This was a sign of deep mourning, used only at times of bereavement or anguish. His words were few and direct: 'God, be merciful to me, a sinner.' There is no sense of his own piety here; only a cry to God for forgiveness in the spirit of the old psalmists (see, for instance, Psalm 51:1). He takes on to himself the name that others, like the Pharisees, fastened on him, 'sinner', acknowledging its accuracy. In the word 'be merciful' it may be that we get a glimpse into what is going on in the Temple, for this can be translated 'be propitiated', 'make an atonement', alluding to the sacrifice there and then being offered in the Temple courts, regarded as the God-appointed means of dealing with sin and maintaining the relationship between God and human beings. In this case it is a cry of longing that *he* be included in the benefits of this sacrifice: 'God, let this atonement be *for me*, a sinner.'

Jesus' conclusion is simple, but undoubtedly shocking for many of his listeners. It was this man, the customs officer, who went home 'justified', rather than the Pharisee. 'Justified' means that *his* prayer was heard and answered; *he* was the one accepted by and acceptable to God; *he* was the one who could truly participate in Israel's hope of God's kingdom. Was this 'justification' something he knew, a confidence he received? Did the Pharisee, correspondingly, leave the Temple courts with a sense of emptiness and futility? Jesus says nothing explicitly about what the men *experienced*. That is not the point of the story. He simply calls his hearers to penetrate the veil of outward appearance and imagine an alternative to received wisdom: imagine that a self-humbling tax collector is acceptable to God whereas a self-confident Pharisee is not. The proverb sums it up: 'all who exalt themselves will be humbled, but all who humble themselves will be exalted'.

As the hearers pondered the story, what would they have thought, in retrospect, of the two characters? As we have seen, the Pharisee's piety was something many would have admired, even if they thought they could never attain such a level of piety themselves. And his prayer would not have had quite the same self-righteous ring as it does to our ears: it was a natural extension of Israel's acute sense of being called to be a special people and echoes verses from the Psalms (such as Psalm 17:3, 4; 26:1, 4–6, 11). But there was another aspect to it. Many would have recognized that there was a dark underside to what the Pharisee was claiming. Luke's Gospel hints that, despite his protestations of righteousness, an element of self-deception – and the attempt to deceive others – was also at work. Each one of the attributes he names was, in fact, twisted in a certain way so that what on the outside appeared to be cleanness and uprightness on the inside was dirty and crooked.

In fact, in Luke 11:39 Jesus directly accuses the Pharisees of 'extortion'. The sting in this accusation was precisely that they *thought* of themselves as set apart from the Gentile practices of flagrant oppression and flaunting of wealth that were enslaving the Jewish people and defiling the land. However, there was another source of oppression for the poor at the time: the Temple itself and the system of tithing associated with it. Not only were ordinary peasants forced to pay exorbitant rents to their rich landlords; they were also bullied by the likes of the Pharisees into a strict observance of the tithing laws, without regard for the mercy that lay at the heart and soul of the Torah, the law God had given to his people for their good. Tithing appeared as a manifestation of a strict devotion to God, but it had, in fact, become a form of oppression. The Pharisee's statement of his own tithing practice is thus seen in a different light. Perhaps *he* did give tithes of all he possessed; but probably not many could afford to. The indictment of Jesus is plainest of all in Luke 11:42. 'Woe to you Pharisees! For you tithe mint and rue and every herb, and neglect justice and the love of God; these you ought to have done, without neglecting the others.' The Pharisee praying in Jesus' story was thankful that he was not 'unrighteous' like others, yet Jesus here accuses the Pharisees of neglecting 'righteousness'. They had a blind spot to their own shortcomings: a practice that they followed as a way of 'righteousness' was a practice that kept others in poverty.

Even the Pharisee's claim that he was not an 'adulterer' like others is seen as questionable in the light of Jesus' remarks elsewhere. In Luke 16:15–18 Jesus warned the Pharisees that their scale of values might not be God's. The Pharisees were eager to 'justify themselves', that is, declare that they were righteous (verse 15), just like this Pharisee in the story. But, says Jesus, what human beings think of as the best thing in the world may yet be abhorrent to God.

The fact that Jesus has to affirm in such strong terms the continued validity of God's ancient law (verse 17) implies that, notwithstanding all their protestations of devotion, the Pharisees were in fact guilty of cheapening or weakening it. It is then that Jesus gives the example of marriage, stating clearly that remarriage after divorce constituted adultery (verse 18). Mark 10:2–9 fills out the picture for us: the Pharisees had made the permission for divorce given in the law (Deuteronomy 24:1) into a charter for easy divorce and remarriage. They did not think of this as adultery. But in Jesus' eyes this was a twisting of the law and a contradiction of the purpose of God in creation.

The Pharisee's prayer, then, was a characteristic piece of self-deception: a parading of what he thought of as his righteousness simply served to mask the truth concerning his actual righteousness. Those who had heard Jesus' sharp words about the Pharisees on other occasions would have recognized the irony in the picture Jesus paints here.

What of the customs officer? The thought of such a person praying in the Temple courts could have been a rather surprising one for Jesus' hearers. Some of them had perhaps become accustomed to Jesus' surprises. They knew the kind of company he kept; they knew that he did not consider himself bound by Pharisaic taboos. But the prayer this social and spiritual outcast prayed would have been striking and memorable, for the key contrast with the Pharisee's prayer is that there is no self-deception. Both are sinners and, in the mercy of God, sin can be forgiven, as the sacrificial system of the Temple, however inadequately, expressed. But the Pharisees – or some of them, at least – instead of letting the law shed light on all the ways in which they fell short of obedience had persuaded themselves (and others) that they were keeping it very satisfactorily. This Pharisee, though, could not persuade God. And God could not 'declare righteous' one who had already declared *himself* righteous on his own terms.

Pharisee and customs officer alike were sinners, not just in the sense of being individual wrongdoers, but in the sense of being caught in systems of injustice: the Pharisee in the matrix of a certain kind of law interpretation that appeared fervently loyal to God, but allowed the laying of burdens on the poor and weak, such as the burden of tithes; the customs officer in the regime of Roman enslavement of the Jewish people. To many, the Pharisee, because of his impressive performance of ritual duties, would have appeared the closer to God, the one who pointed the way by which Israel might find salvation and rescue. But some Pharisees, it seems, had made the fatal mistake of thinking they were no longer in need of the penetrating critique, correction and forgiveness of God. So it was left, remarkably, to a worldly customs officer to show the way and pray the exemplary, painfully straightforward, prayer: God, have mercy on me, a sinner.

13

Unpayable Debt

The Unforgiving Servant:
Matthew 18:21–35

Then Peter came and said to him, 'Lord, if another member of the church sins against me, how often should I forgive? As many as seven times?' Jesus said to him, 'Not seven times, but, I tell you, seventy-seven times. For this reason the kingdom of heaven may be compared to a king who wished to settle accounts with his slaves. When he began the reckoning, one who owed him ten thousand talents was brought to him; and, as he could not pay, his lord ordered him to be sold, together with his wife and children and all his possessions, and payment to be made. So the slave fell on his knees before him, saying, "Have patience with me, and I will pay you everything." And out of pity for him, the lord of that slave released him and forgave him the debt. But that same slave, as he went out, came upon one of his fellow slaves who owed him a hundred denarii; and seizing him by the throat, he said, "Pay what you owe." Then his fellow slave fell down and pleaded with him, "Have patience with me, and I will pay you." But he refused; then he went and threw him into prison until he would pay the debt. When his fellow slaves saw what had happened, they were greatly distressed, and they went and reported to their lord all that had taken place. Then his lord summoned him and said to

him, "You wicked slave! I forgave you all that debt because
you pleaded with me. Should you not have had mercy on your
fellow slave, as I had mercy on you?" And in anger his lord
handed him over to be tortured until he would pay his entire
debt. So my heavenly Father will also do to every one of you, if
you do not forgive your brother or sister from your heart.'

A crisis of debt bedevils relationships between the rich and
poor world's in the twenty-first century, as well as affecting
many less-well-off individuals in the rich world. A similar
crisis is reflected in the relationships between different
members of the social hierarchy seen in this tale from the
first century. It reminds us that debt is not just a matter of
cold financial facts in an account book. It is an aspect of
human interaction, which can result from an exercise of
overweening power, and end in the loss of all freedom.
The 'slaves' here are the trusted bureaucrats of a king, not
poor tenant farmers. But, though invisible, the peasants
play a crucial part in the narrative for, undoubtedly, it is
by exacting exorbitant tribute that the king amassed his
fantastic wealth.

This story is set by Matthew in the context of a question
to Jesus from Peter about the limits of forgiveness. It is a
question that reflects a concern of the early church: given the
continued weakness of the new community and its members
and the inevitable lapses into habits of life that belonged
to the days before God's kingdom dawned – disputes,
bickering, resentments and selfish pride – could, and should,
the members really go on forgiving one another? Jesus'
answer is uncompromising: one should forgive not merely
up to seven times but up to seventy times seven – in other
words, indefinitely.

The parable backs up the message, though, as we shall
see, not in the straightforward way often suggested. But,
like the other stories of Jesus, it is far more than straight

moral exhortation in fancy dress. It asks listeners to imagine a world where things are surprisingly different from their usual experience: where a mighty lord writes off an almost incredibly large debt. Characteristically, it focuses on a concrete social and economic issue. The debts in the story are real monetary debts. Already in the time of Jesus 'debt' could be used as a metaphor for 'sin'; but 'forgiveness' would not usually have been seen in abstract terms as the mere restoration of feelings of good will. God's forgiveness of his people would be seen, it was believed, through signs of security and prosperity in their land. People's forgiveness of one another would be shown in tangible ways, above all in the release of burdensome debt. One of the great liberating provisions of the law was the year of 'Jubilee' every fifty years when property was to be returned to its original owners (Leviticus 25:8–17). Whether this command was ever seriously carried out is disputed. But it remained a vision that ran right against the practice of ever-increasing concentration of the land in the hands of the few: a time when the misery and indignity of being, in essence, the property of another could cease, and a fresh start be made.

When Jesus says 'the kingdom of heaven may be compared to a king who ...' he is not, of course, attempting an awkward comparison between a kingdom and a king. He is saying that the whole sequence of events depicted in the story somehow reflects and represents the way things work under God's rule. This means too that we are warned off any notion that the king in the story directly reflects God. It is precisely a *human* king whom the audience is meant to envisage. Similarly, at the end of the story when Jesus says 'So my heavenly Father will also do to every one of you, if ...' we are not to imagine that the punishment meted out by the king on the unforgiving servant directly reflects the kind of justice executed by God upon the unforgiving. It is rather that, as in many another tale of Jesus, the story in its entire shape hints at the both wondrous and urgent order of God's kingdom. This order is not something that exists in a vague ethereal way, in some distant future or unseen world or inner state of mind, but something that can be glimpsed in everyday life in both the surprising compassion and the ruthless punishment of a fickle king.

This is one of only three stories of Jesus to revolve around a 'king'. Maybe that is precisely because he saw the danger that his audiences might jump too quickly to the conclusion that he was asserting a similarity between the kind of kings they were familiar with and God. Be that as it may, the 'kings' who would immediately have leapt into their minds were the Herod family, self-indulgent and often cruel puppet rulers over Palestine, or parts of it, under the Romans. As we have seen already, these rulers, together with a small number of other aristocrats, had taken many of the populace into virtual slavery by buying up more and more land and forcing small farmers into working it as tenants, paying huge rents out of the yield of the ground. Trusted 'slaves' of the rulers, officials who benefited considerably from their masters' wealth and prestige while remaining far below them in social status, would be responsible for collecting the revenues. From time to time there would be a day of reckoning when the king called his officials in to hand over what they had collected.

Such a day of reckoning is portrayed here and Jesus' hearers would have known exactly the kind of event he was referring to. The attention gathers on one particular 'slave' who owed 'ten thousand talents'. It seems that this king in his fantastic wealth had been very relaxed about keeping the accounts up to date. The amount was truly exorbitant, comparable to the annual returns from whole swathes of the empire to Rome. There is probably more than a touch of humorous exaggeration here, but the sum is also a reminder of the extraordinary riches accumulated by a few.

The retainer, banking on his lord's indulgence, has been gradually feathering his nest, enjoying a little luxury. But he has gone too far. When the king demands his revenues they are not there to hand over. So the king orders him to be sold along with his family and all his possessions. In other words, the man himself will become another's possession, along with all his assets, human and material. From being a high-ranking 'slave', with responsibilities and privileges that would have been the envy of many a free man, he faces the prospect of becoming, with his family, a much more menial functionary with a known track record of embezzlement. Only thus could 'payment' to the king be made, though with such a large debt there is surely a trace of irony: even the price gained from his sale into 'slavery' would never pay it off.

There is a wry playfulness to the next moment of the drama. The man falls down in a sign of obeisance before the king and begs him to have patience – he would pay everything! Jesus and the audience, and the imaginary king, would know that this was quite impossible. But this is a picture of a desperate man, desperate in the manner of the widow shamelessly pestering the judge, or the prodigal son pleading to be a hired servant. One would not expect cool negotiation in such circumstances. He is casting himself on the mercy of the king, saying anything that might make the king favourable towards him. The level of freedom and honour and trust he has so far enjoyed are so precious that he will humble himself before the one in whose hands his future lies so that he might retain them.

So comes the first great surprise of the story. The king, now being referred to as 'lord', accentuating the master–slave relationship, was 'moved with compassion'. This word for a deep 'gut feeling' towards someone is used in other stories: of the Samaritan seeing the wounded man and of the father seeing his wayward son. These are all turning points, moments of shock, relief and hope. The picture of a Samaritan showing compassion to a Jew or a good Jewish father showing compassion to a defiled, rebellious spend-thrift would have struck Jesus' hearers as highly unex-pected, but the picture of a vain Herod being moved by the situation of a fawning bureaucrat would have been more unexpected still. The king had the man set free and absolved him of the debt.

But the story is not over and the next twist is like a twist of the knife. As the compassion of the prodigal's father is followed by the anger of his brother, so here, but still more painfully, remarkable forgiveness is followed by extra-ordinary vengefulness. The scene shifts outside the king's court. The retainer, having against all expectation retained his basic freedom, goes out and finds a fellow slave. Did he just bump into him or did he go looking for him? The point is not stressed, but it is interesting to speculate. One gets the impression of a habitually bullying character. This fellow slave owed him a sum of a hundred denarii. By comparison with the amount of debt from which the first slave had just been released, this was a tiny sum, but it was not trivial. A day labourer would have been lucky to earn it in a year. We must remember that the king had not made the forgiven slave rich; he had just given him a clean slate. After a period of living it up on borrowed credit he now found himself in a newly tight financial situation. Apparently he has no qualms about doing just what he might have done had he never even come before the king. Taking his fellow slave by the throat, he demands payment of the debt.

The other slave's reaction as it is recounted is almost identical to that of the first slave in front of the king. He falls down and begs him to have patience, promising to pay up. But the first slave is having none of it. Unlike the king, he does not have the power to sell his colleague, but he can

get him thrown into prison as a debtor. That is just what
he does.

The parable has delivered a double shock. The king, the
distant, famously cold, uncaring potentate at the very top
of the social pile, has been touched with pity and acted
generously. But the retainer, far from learning from the
king's example, has remained heartless and mean. In times
of economic stress, tight possessiveness and indeed violence
are never far away.

At this point other slaves come on to the stage. This
group – probably knowing of the king's act of mercy – are
very distressed at their fellow servant's lack of it and go to
report what he has done. They see the terrible injustice of a
refusal to forgive when so much has been forgiven; still
more, they seem to see the unnaturalness of the slave's
action, his failure to catch on to the new spirit of forgiveness
the king has initiated. So the slave is summoned a second
time to the court.

Calling him 'wicked', the king puts the simple question
to him: should you not have forgiven your fellow slave as I
forgave you? The master storyteller leaves the question
hanging: no answer is put into the slave's mouth. But here is
the third and final and terrible twist. It has angered the
king that one should so fail to register, or be moved by,
generosity shown. He consigns the slave to a worse fate
than either being sold in ignominy to a stranger or being
consigned to the common debtors' prison. Instruments of
torture were sadly familiar in the ancient world, as they still
are. The slave is to be tortured until that surely illusory day
when the debt should be paid.

It strikes a modern reader, as it might well have struck
an ancient hearer, that this is a chilling end to the story.
The king seems to have done a volte-face. Where is his
compassion now? This fact serves to emphasize again the

humanness of the characters and the danger of drawing too close an analogy between the king's behaviour and that of God. This changeable king is precisely the kind of weak and vacillating individual that Herod Antipas appears in the Gospels to have been (see the way he treated John the Baptist, recorded in Mark 6:14–29: he admired him but had him beheaded in response to a request from his wife, via his daughter, at a party where he did not want to lose honour among his guests). Like other figures in Jesus' parables he is quite clearly *not* presented as having undergone a profound inner conversion. We remember how the shrewd manager's employer knows which side his bread is buttered and therefore affirms the manager's tactics of debt remission; how the judge wants to stop being hassled and therefore delivers a just verdict. The king in this story was moved to show mercy, but that does not make him either saintly or consistent. He seems to regret his moment of vulnerability. The slave's utter refusal to follow suit brings shame on him. To see his generosity thrown back in his face causes the king to revert to type and respond with violence and cruelty.

The ruthlessness of his response suggests that he had not intended that act of mercy to have been an isolated incident. He had meant it to set in train a new way of life and business in which forgiveness, not foreclosure, was the order of the day, and in which the vicious process of exploitation, spiralling down through the layers of the social hierarchy, might be ended, and one might not only receive one's own freedom but give others theirs. Perhaps he had in fact glimpsed that to wipe the slate of debt clean all round would lead to a better, safer life for the entire community. Perhaps he had decided, in a small but significant way, to proclaim the Jubilee. But his retainer had utterly failed to catch on.

For Jesus' hearers there was a clear warning here: not to trifle with the patience of unpredictable rulers. Especially, to treat a gesture of kindness so ungratefully, and to resort to violence, is seen as inevitably leading to punishment. Notwithstanding the charges of sedition on which he himself was eventually handed over to the Roman authorities, Jesus consistently warned *against* rebellion. He was shrewd enough to see its folly. But what he could also see was the kingdom of God breaking in and taking effect right in the heart of the most unpropitious-seeming human regime. The great day of Jubilee, the time for the forgiveness of debts, *had* dawned. So there is not only warning in the story, but the encouragement to look for the signs of hope. Not only was rebellion bad policy, it was also unnecessary, because even in the house of Herod – conceivably – the signs of the kingdom might be seen! A spirit of forgiveness might be found breaking out in the most unlikely quarters. And the way to show, in practice, that one expected God's kingdom, believed in it, wanted to see it extended, was not – as many thought – the way of violence or the way of ever-stricter enforcement of law. It was certainly not the 'me first' possessive mentality, which involved first living off the largesse of a rich lord and then the imprisonment of a fellow slave for the sake of a debt. It was the way of forgiveness: costly, practical, generous – and endless.

But, finally, what of that concluding sentence about Jesus' 'heavenly Father'? Does it not really seem as if Jesus' Father is being compared, whether by Jesus or by Matthew, to a cruel and fickle Herod? The very obvious national and human connotations of the story – not to mention the awe in which the unseen God, who forbade images of himself to be made, was held – mean that the first hearers would have been very unlikely to have drawn such a crudely close comparison, just as Jesus would have been very unlikely to have intended it. However, a comparison of some kind there undoubtedly is. Jesus is saying that the warning inherent in the parable applies to all who nurture a possessive and demanding rather than a forgiving and releasing heart. But this is not because they will fall victim directly to some vindictive supernatural version of Herod after death. It is rather that God's judgement will be worked out *through* the Herods and their like, just as these rulers may also, surprisingly, be agents of God's mercy. And for God's people to fight one another would be as foolish and as futile as to fight their overlords. Sadly, both happened in the rebellion and internecine strife of the Jewish War, 66–70 CE. Disaster did indeed strike when the Romans came to destroy Jerusalem. Like Jeremiah of old, calling on his people to submit to the enemy as the agent of judgement and so more quickly find the mercy of God, so Jesus called the people of his day to see this extraordinary, unthinkable truth: that their alien rulers were the agents of God's kingdom, to judge but also to save.

14

Seasonal Survival

The Labourers in the Vineyard:
Matthew 20:1–16

'For the kingdom of heaven is like a landowner who went out early in the morning to hire labourers for his vineyard. After agreeing with the labourers for the usual daily wage, he sent them into his vineyard. When he went out about nine o'clock, he saw others standing idle in the marketplace; and he said to them, "You also go into the vineyard, and I will pay you whatever is right." So they went. When he went out again about noon and about three o'clock, he did the same. And about five o'clock he went out and found others standing around; and he said to them, "Why are you standing here idle all day?" They said to him, "Because no one has hired us." He said to them, "You also go into the vineyard." When evening came, the owner of the vineyard said to his manager, "Call the labourers and give them their pay, beginning with the last and then going to the first." When those hired about five o'clock came, each of them received the usual daily wage. Now when the first came, they thought they would receive more; but each of them also received the usual daily wage. And when they received it, they grumbled against the landowner, saying, "These last worked only one hour, and you have made them equal to us who have borne the burden of the day and the scorching heat." But he replied to one of them, "Friend, I am doing you no wrong; did you not agree with me for the usual daily wage? Take what belongs to you and go; I choose to give to this last the same as I give to you. Am I not allowed to do what I choose with what belongs to me? Or are you envious because I am generous?" So the last will be first, and the first will be last.'

The workers in this story were among the most insecure members of society. 'Day-labouring' in harvest seasons was the employment sought by those who had no family land of their own to till, no trade to ply. The size both of families and of the rents and taxes that ate up their livelihood may well have driven them from their homes. But at harvest time extra hands were needed. This was their opportunity to earn some kind of meagre living of their own. The rest of the year, probably, they would have to survive on others' kindness or sense of duty; many may have turned to beggary or thieving.

This tale of a day in the marketplace and vineyard is presented by Jesus as another glimpse of the kingdom of 'heaven', the reality of God's rule. It starts with a man who is a 'householder', the master of a large estate. It is the season for gathering grapes and he needs extra workers for the burdensome task of picking them from the vines and treading them in the winepress. So he goes out early in the morning to the marketplace of the local village, the place where the would-be labourers hung around. It seems unlikely that this was normal practice: the landowner has a steward, as we later discover – might we not have expected the steward to be charged with taking on the casual labourers for the day? Perhaps we are being alerted already to the fact that this is a rather unusual householder. Anyway, he agrees, apparently, to take on all those who were in the square at that point and settles with them a wage of a denarius for the day. This was a standard daily sum for a labourer, though it was barely a subsistence wage. He sets them to work in his vineyard.

This is indeed an active and proactive employer. It would be important to harvest the grapes quickly, when they were ripe enough to be picked, but before they grew over-ripe and rotted on the vines. He needs more pickers so he goes out again into the marketplace 'at the third hour' (about nine in the morning). More expectant candidates have arrived by then, and they also are hired. This time a specific wage is not mentioned: the landowner just assures them that he will give them 'whatever is right'. He has further trips at noon and at three in the afternoon.

The task is urgent, unfinished and needs yet more hands. So at 'the eleventh hour', at five in the afternoon, shortly before the day's work has to end when the sun goes down, the owner goes out for a final visit to the village square. Here he finds still more candidates. He is puzzled that they are there and asks them why they have been standing there all day not doing anything. (The use of the word 'idle' implies to us that he is accusing them of laziness, but this is not the necessary implication.) Surely, he implies, there will have been other vineyard owners on the lookout for day labourers? 'No one has taken us on' is the rather pitiful reply. Had they really been there all day, but the landowner had not noticed them on his earlier visits? Or had they just appeared after three, having wandered from village to village without success? There is still an hour's working time left and the owner sends them too into his vineyard.

Sunset comes and the work must stop. The owner summons his steward, who has charge of the money, and tells him to pay the workers. (A different word is used for this official from that used for the manager who was sacked in another story, but the two men may have had similar roles.) He adds a special requirement: the steward is to start with those who were taken on last. The steward obediently starts paying out the wages. Those hired at five in the afternoon receive a denarius – the amount agreed with the first hired. We are left to assume that those hired during the day also received this amount. The scene shifts to the payment of those hired at daybreak. Having seen what the others had received, they expect to receive more than the promised denarius, but they get the same.

The householder, apparently, has been watching the proceedings; at least, he is not far away. He is a hands-on type. It is to him, directly, that the first workers address their complaint. They somehow know that *he* is responsible; this is not some mean trick of the steward's. It seems so unjust: they have done twelve hours' work, under the scorching sun, and they have been paid no more than those who just turned up for an hour before twilight.

The householder's response is gentle, measured and reasonable. He is not the same sort of character as the fickle king in the preceding story. He addresses one of the workers personally – presumably their spokesman, the *ad hoc* 'shop steward' – calling him 'friend', a well-intentioned way of speaking to someone whose name one did not know. He affirms that he is doing him no *wrong*. This word is related to the one he used when he promised to give those hired later in the day what was 'right'. From his perspective he has dealt justly with *all* his workers. He continues: 'Did you not agree with me for a denarius?' This was the normal daily wage; they had not demurred at being hired for that amount – indeed anything extra would have been considered unusually generous. Now the tone turns to one of more direct rebuke. 'Take what belongs to you and go; I choose to give to this last the same as I give to you. Am I not allowed to do what I choose with what belongs to me?' He emphasizes that he is not acting to deprive the first workers but to be generous towards the later ones. He is being unjust to no one in giving the expected daily wage; he is free to give *more* than what might have been expected to those who had only worked for an hour. The closing question goes to the heart of the issue: 'Are you envious because I am generous?' Like the unforgiving servant in the previous story it seems as if these workers had not caught on to the spirit of the master.

Two implications of this scene are interesting to ponder. First, the master quite deliberately ordered the wages to be paid first to those hired last. He obviously intended his attitude and policy to be known to those who had worked longer; he was not interested, at least on this occasion, in secret generosity. He hoped, indeed, that something of this spirit *would* catch on. Second, the master has no need to tell the steward what to pay each worker. Of course, this omission may simply be due to conciseness in storytelling, but it seems significant. The steward knew the master's mind. We are left wondering whether this was what the master did *every* day during the harvest season, and, this time, he wanted all the workers to know it.

What would the significance of the master's action have been for Jesus' hearers? They would have known that, that night, *all* the day labourers would have been able to buy at least some food for the coming day. They had all received a day's wage. They had been paid not according to hours worked but according to their need for survival.

Although it is possible to read this landowner as a cynical type, treating his workforce with contempt, it is probably better to take him at his word. Certainly he is a man of the world. He is 'generous' not in an extravagant, revolutionary way, turning paupers into rich men, but within the bounds of the existing social structures. It would have made little difference to his own coffers whether he paid the workers a denarius or a twelfth of a denarius, just as the king who released a servant from a debt would hardly have noticed the difference, even though it was a debt of ten thousand talents. But, rather than being pernickety about calculating an hourly rate, he paid them what they needed.

It is important to see, though, that this was more than generosity. It was also *justice* in a profoundly biblical sense. The master himself, as we have seen, promises to give the various workers what is 'right' or 'just' and asserts that he has done the first workers no 'wrong'. The justice that God had commanded and exemplified in Old Testament times went beyond the arraignment and punishment of law-breakers. It was the positive, active quality of seeking out and setting right the fundamental wrongs of society that deprived some people of the basic necessities for the enjoyment of life. It was not the same as modern egalitarianism, which strives for 'equality' in every respect between members of society, but it was especially focused on the poor and needy. For they were precisely the victims of *injustice*, an injustice deeply rooted in the structures of society, which required positive action to reverse.

Some today may be suspicious of this notion, as if it romanticizes the poor, or removes from them all responsibility for their own lives. In this connection it is worth stressing that the Old Testament would have no truck with the kind of partiality that let a criminal off the hook simply because he was poor. Wrongdoing was to be punished whoever the wrongdoer was. The obligation to keep the commandments of God was the same whatever one's wealth or social status. This is clearly reiterated by Jesus. The sharp challenge of many of his stories – like this one – is precisely to the poor. Will they, despite their poverty, adopt an attitude of forgiveness and generosity, or will they turn to possessiveness and violence?

Yet the Bible forbids us from turning a blind eye to the fact that injustice is far more than the wrongdoing of individuals. It is a corporate reality, wedded to the truth that members of the human race, in biblical terms, are

profoundly interconnected. Doing *justice* is therefore far
more than keeping on the right side of the law. It is seeking
actively to reverse those conditions, arising from cumula-
tive human selfishness, which deprive many of human
dignity. Jesus' stories help his hearers to start to imagine
simple, concrete ways in which this might happen. So here
we should not focus on the supposed 'idleness' of the
workers hired last, vaguely imagining that they had been
lying in bed all day instead of out 'on their bikes' looking
for work. We should focus rather on the ugly injustice of a
society where exorbitant rents and taxes drove many to
the very edge of existence. And the act of the master should
be seen not so much as magnanimity to the undeserving but
as the first stirrings of justice to the poor. A denarius a day
was precious little, but for the surprised folk who had only
been able to get an hour's work, it might have kept body
and soul together a little longer.

But could such a thing have happened? Were there such
landowners around? Would such a society in which all
people received their basic needs have appeared just a vain
pipe dream to those who listened to Jesus?

Telling a story like this would, once more, have opened a
chink of light on a grim and often desperate situation. For
any landowners who happened to be listening – even King
Herod, after all, was anxious to see Jesus (Luke 9:9) – the
story would certainly have offered a clear challenge: one
that many might have ignored, but one that some might
have heeded. But more than this, Jesus' implication – made
clear in the introductory words – is that *God's kingdom of
justice is indeed dawning*. A world is coming into being
where such things can happen and will happen. And his
hearers of all kinds can catch the spirit that is in the air. In
this tale, like that of the unforgiving servant, underdogs are
invited to imitate the attitude that – surprisingly for some –

is being shown by some of their rich masters. In another story, that of the shrewd manager, the converse happens: a rich man is seen latching on to the wisdom of debt remission exemplified by one of his officials. God is at work in these people who suddenly discover the just way, whether they know it or not, whether they stick to it or not. Those who see the signs will find that the way is both wise and possible, however contrary to accepted practice it runs.

The final comment added to the parable is a theme running like a thread through the Gospels: 'So the last shall be first, and the first last.' It picks up on the order in which the workers were paid, but in the context of the story its reference goes much wider than that. The rule of God entails reversals of all kinds – not least reversal of fortune for those whose very life is daily under threat. This is not the sadly familiar phenomenon of human revolutions in which the oppressed very quickly turn into the oppressors and the rich and the poor simply swap places. This is God's kingdom, in which human beings are reconciled to each other; where – for example, and just as a start – a prosperous landowner gives his day labourers what they need, not what they have worked for, and where (perhaps) they may share their pleasure graciously with one another.

15

Murderous Revolt

The Wicked Tenants:
Mark 12:1–12
(see also Matthew 21:33–46; Luke 20:9–18)

Then he began to speak to them in parables. 'A man planted a vineyard, put a fence around it, dug a pit for the wine press, and built a watchtower; then he leased it to tenants and went to another country. When the season came, he sent a slave to the tenants to collect from them his share of the produce of the vineyard. But they seized him, and beat him, and sent him away empty-handed. And again he sent another slave to them; this one they beat over the head and insulted. Then he sent another, and that one they killed. And so it was with many others; some they beat, and others they killed. He had still one other, a beloved son. Finally he sent him to them, saying, "They will respect my son." But those tenants said to one another, "This is the heir; come, let us kill him, and the inheritance will be ours." So they seized him, killed him, and threw him out of the vineyard. What then will the owner of the vineyard do? He will come and destroy the tenants and give the vineyard to others. Have you not read this scripture: "The stone that the builders rejected has become the cornerstone; this was the Lord's doing, and it is amazing in our eyes"?' When they realized that he had told this parable against them, they wanted to arrest him, but they feared the crowd. So they left him and went away.

Here is another story about a vineyard. This time the focus is not on a single day at harvest time, with a landowner intimately and surprisingly involved in the proceedings. The story covers a longer period of time, and the landlord is absent, unable to supervise transactions or enforce his will. It is also one of the bleakest of Jesus' tales in its prophetic overtones of impending judgement.

The situation, like that of all the tales, was well known. Those who owned most of the land of Israel in the time of Jesus were not the Israelites to whom the land had been passed down from generation to generation. They were mainly members of the conquering Roman race, or others of mixed blood, descended in part from the Hellenic rulers who had preceded the Romans in dominating that part of the Near East. Since such foreign landlords often had many large estates, and many of them had come from other parts of the Roman Empire, they might frequently be absent. As we have already seen, this ruling élite imposed a more and more crushing burden of rent and taxation on the native population. When a peasant farmer could no longer afford the rent his land was appropriated. He was allowed to live on a part of the yield, but the rest was due to the landowner. Such seizure of land was not a recent phenomenon, nor one practised only by foreign powers – King Ahab of Israel had taken the vineyard of Naboth (1 Kings 21).

For Jesus' hearers, then, the story does not start in innocent peacefulness. Behind the picture of a man planting a vineyard and letting it out to 'tenants' there is no comfortable scenario of modern middle-class capitalism. Rather, there are overtones of force and oppression. When we think of 'tenants' of a piece of land we may be inclined to think of gardeners in rented allotments growing fruit and vegetables. These tenants are different. They are effectively slaves on their own territory. Being in the vineyard is not a hobby. Its yield means life, but, unfortunately, most of it must go to the landowner. At harvest time the due proportion of the grapes would be sent for. This would, no doubt, be sold for cash to finance the landowner's luxurious lifestyle or military adventures (as we shall see in the next story, such people often kept private armies).

This landowner had taken care to establish a productive vineyard. He planted it, put a protective hedge around it, dug a pit for the winepress and built a watchtower (an important item when, as we have seen in another story, sabotage of other people's land was a regular occurrence). He would not have done all this himself; the language is shorthand for 'caused to be planted' and so on. The interesting thing about this picture is its close resemblance to the 'Song of the Vineyard' in the book of Isaiah the prophet (chapter 5). There, the planting of a vineyard was a picture of the Lord's establishment of his people, Israel. As we shall see, this is a highly significant element of the background to this story.

The time for the landowner's collection of his share of the produce arrived. He sent a 'slave' or 'bondservant' to get it. 'Slaves' of this kind were highly responsible middlemen, such as we have already met. Like the customs officers, they would have been mainly Jews who wanted to escape from the increasing penury of ordinary peasant life by entering the bureaucracy of the rulers, even if it meant leaving behind many scruples about observance of the law. When the slave arrives we see straightaway that the tenants are in no mood to comply. They are in rebellion. It seems that they have had enough of their miserable existence and their increasing deprivation of land, livelihood and freedom.

Taking advantage of the landowner's absence, they beat up the slave and send him away with nothing.

The different versions of the story recount the next stage with some variations on the number of slaves and the kind of treatment they received. Sticking to Mark's version, we find another slave being sent, and being wounded in the head and degraded (in precisely what way is left to the imagination). A third slave was killed. Many others came and suffered either murder or grievous bodily harm. Clearly, the tenants were determined to repossess the land. Their desperation and the vulnerability of the messengers drove them to take extraordinary risks, perhaps increasingly scenting victory. Jesus' listeners would have heard of such rebellions.

The landowner may have been a tyrant in an oppressive system, but he exercises remarkable restraint. He persists in giving his tenants the chance to comply with his requirement. He does not, of course, come in person; the lives of several members of his staff are sacrificed. But then he takes a great gamble. The person to whom one could delegate authority most completely was a son. Operating, it seems, with a commendable dependence on personal authority rather than brute force, perhaps even with the idea of entering into negotiations, he sends his beloved son. They will respect him, he thinks.

They do not. They take this as their golden opportunity. Recognizing the young man, thinking that his father the landowner must be dead, and hardly believing their luck and his folly, it seems to them that the son's life is all that stands between them and repossession of the inheritance. They therefore take him, kill him, and throw his body triumphantly out of the vineyard.

Unlike many of Jesus' stories, this one has an ending that would have been entirely expected by his hearers. Indeed, in Matthew's account of its telling, when Jesus asks 'What will the owner of the vineyard do?' he leaves the hearers to give the answer, which they do correctly. Everyone knows what a landowner in that society would do in that situation. There would be no clemency now. He would bring down the might of his armed men upon the rebels. They would be killed, and the vineyard would be let out to others, who would already have received the strongest possible warning of the price of non-compliance.

Here, then, is another warning to the people of the folly of rebellion. Note that, as in several other parables, it is not only rebellion of servants or tenants against a master that is at issue. It is also the attitude of the underlings to other underlings. The shrewd manager gave an example of generous dealing to other subordinates. But we have also seen the unforgiving servant, the grumbling day-labourers, and now murderous tenants, who, before they killed the heir, killed a number of more lowly ambassadors. A situation of despair can all too easily lead to a culture of violence. Jesus' warning is that it simply will not pay.

Note as well, however, the hints that the landowner is not as unreasonable as he may stereotypically have been expected to be or as the tenants may have imagined him. His sending of endless embassies, and the final extraordinary risk of sending his son, indicate an openness and patience that is perhaps surprising. It is the same kind of surprise that we find in the king who let off the debt or the master who paid the daily wage to all; though, as with the king, the refusal to catch the spirit is swiftly and harshly dealt with. Jesus seems to be offering another characteristic glimpse of the kingdom. Look around, he says, and, if you have eyes to see, you will see that all is not as bleak as you think. You do not have to resort to violence, but if you do, it will go ill for you.

It is not surprising that Matthew, Mark and Luke all record that the Jewish leaders perceived that Jesus had told this parable against them. Nor is it surprising that Matthew should record in this context that the people generally considered Jesus a 'prophet', for this was indeed speech in the style of the old prophets, warning of disaster if the path of violence and rebellion was followed. Especially, it resonated with the message of Jeremiah, who had urged his people to *submit* to their mighty conquering enemy, for that would be the way of peace. The enemy was the agent of God's own judgement upon them.

The Jewish leaders would not have been slow to recognize in the opening of the story the echoes of the 'Song of the Vineyard' in Isaiah 5. That recognition would have stung, for that too was a prophecy of judgement on Israel, the Lord's carefully tended vineyard. Isaiah's parable is somewhat different from that of Jesus: in Isaiah, it is a fruitless vineyard that symbolizes Israel's lack of response to God's tender care. But for Isaiah, as well as Jesus, the heart of the condition for which judgement comes is *violence*. 'He looked for justice, but behold, bloodshed; for righteousness, but behold, a cry!' (Isaiah 5:7).

In Isaiah's time Israel was not yet overrun by foreign powers. Many in Jesus' day perhaps thought that in a situation of subservience to Roman might violence was justified, even if it had not been justified previously. Jesus' parable tenderly and tragically points to another reading of current affairs. Alien landlords now in actual practice played the role of the Lord, the 'beloved' of Isaiah's song, digging and guarding the vineyards. But the warrant for rebellion was no greater than if Israel's Master had been the owner; and the folly of it was as large. Members of the covenant family, subordinates of the foreign power, would suffer. And when eventually the rebels' attack was directed against the supreme landowner himself, the Roman Emperor, disaster would come crashing down. The Lord's cause would not be served by a fierce defence of national independence. On the contrary, his judgement would be seen in the continued rule of the foreigners who owned the vine-yards, and in their letting out of the lands to other tenants.

Such a message would have stung and infuriated the Jewish leaders. They, of course, were not those plotting violent uprising – that was left to the rougher terrorist types. But they heard the prophetic word and its implication that a day would come in which the rule of the Romans would be extended rather than shaken off; in which the limited freedom and independence they now enjoyed would be drastically curtailed; and which all their cunning policies would be incapable of stopping. The Sadducees' cosy rela-tionship with the Roman regime and the Pharisees' attempt to bring in the kingdom of God through stricter law obser-vance would both fail. Neither accommodation to the rich and powerful, nor angular self-assertion through the purity regulations, nor armed revolt would bring in that kingdom. The kingdom was coming, but it would come as blessing only to those who submitted to the will of God, revealed in Jesus.

So this is a story of reversal in which those who had what they believed to be an inalienable right to the land are warned of destruction if they seek to overthrow their oppressors with violence. As underdogs they may have been sorely provoked, but the warning is uncompromising. The land would be given to 'others'. This reversal is expressed in the quotation from Psalm 118:22 about the 'rejected stone' becoming the 'head of the corner'. An apparently misshapen and useless building block is suddenly just the right stone for a crucial position. Originally, this seems to have been a saying expressing the wonderful reversal whereby tiny Israel herself, or a humble tribe or individual within Israel, had been exalted by God to a place of honour and triumph. Now it appears wryly in the mouth of Jesus as a comment on the parable, suggesting that the 'rejected'

Gentiles, epitomized in the landowners and their collaborating slaves, regarded as defiled and beyond the pale by many, were the ones who would be victorious. In Matthew the implication is made explicit, drawing again on the metaphorical language of Isaiah: 'Therefore I tell you, the kingdom of God will be taken away from you and given to a nation producing the fruits of it' (21:43). This does not mean that the Jewish race were now forever to be excluded from God's kingdom. It does mean that, for Jesus and the early Christians, a line had been crossed: no longer were the privileges of being God's people – including the very land itself – seen as the automatic birthright of a race, but as the possession of all who bore the 'fruit' of peaceful justice.

16

Vacant Places

The Wedding of the King's Son:
Matthew 22:1–14

Once more Jesus spoke to them in parables, saying: 'The kingdom of heaven may be compared to a king who gave a wedding banquet for his son. He sent his slaves to call those who had been invited to the wedding banquet, but they would not come. Again he sent other slaves, saying, "Tell those who have been invited: Look, I have prepared my dinner, my oxen and my fat calves have been slaughtered, and everything is ready; come to the wedding banquet." But they made light of it and went away, one to his farm, another to his business, while the rest seized his slaves, mistreated them, and killed them. The king was enraged. He sent his troops, destroyed those murderers, and burned their city. Then he said to his slaves, "The wedding is ready, but those invited were not worthy. Go therefore into the main streets, and invite everyone you find to the wedding banquet." Those slaves went out into the streets and gathered all whom they found, both good and bad; so the wedding hall was filled with guests. But when the king came in to see the guests, he noticed a man there who was not wearing a wedding robe, and he said to him, "Friend, how did you get in here without a wedding robe?" And he was speechless. Then the king said to the attendants, "Bind him hand and foot, and throw him into the outer darkness, where there will be weeping and gnashing of teeth." For many are called, but few are chosen.'

The marriage of a king's son would have been a great occasion. The people of Palestine would no doubt have been able to think of a number of such weddings in the Herod family over the years. These would have been opportunities for the king to display his magnificence and generosity as well as cement a convenient family alliance. They would have been opportunities, also, to keep the invited members of the aristocracy in a state of indebtedness to the king, and thus maintain the delicate balance of honour and power so central to a stratified society and to the perpetuation of his own position. But all of these satisfactory outcomes would be frustrated if the invited guests failed to appear.

This is the situation that lies behind this story in Matthew. The hearers would have expected the guest list to include all the 'great and good' of the land. This would, of course, have meant many of the influential Jews in the priestly hierarchy and in other positions of favour with Rome, as well as Roman landowners and aristocrats of mixed race like Herod himself.

The day of the wedding drew near and, according to custom, responsible officials were sent out to escort the guests to the palace in time to enjoy the freshly cooked meal. Astonishingly, they would not come. One can imagine at least a smirk on the faces of the audience at the picture of a Herod being snubbed in this fashion. The king sends out a second team of officials with a fuller, more enticing version of the reminder: 'The dinner is ready; all the animals have been killed; everything has been prepared.' (The scale of the event, with numerous 'oxen and fatted calves', contrasts with the much humbler celebration for the return of the prodigal, for which the family's sole 'fatted calf' was killed.) But the response is no more positive. Many of the guests shrug off the summons and carry on as if nothing is happening, attending to the business of their estates, or their trading in the marketplace. Some are abusive to the king's messengers, even resorting to violence and murder. This is clearly a king who is widely disrespected, even hated. There seems to be a concerted plan to show him that he is no longer held in honour, that his authority is not acknowledged.

Jesus' listeners would not have been at all surprised to hear him describe the king's reaction. It is as swift and ruthless as that of the king who forgave a debtor but then discovered the debtor's unforgiving spirit. In his anger the king sends out his private posses of troops to put an end to the rebels and burn their town (apparently the home of the most murderous of the invitees). Some consider this part of the story so implausible that it must be a direct reference (probably inserted after the event) to the destruction of Jerusalem in 70 CE. But many aristocrats had private armies, and it is not in the least unlikely that a king such as Herod, treated in such a way, would have responded like this. It is pedantic to think of this all happening while the dinner was getting cold: timing is not at issue here – Jesus is simply finishing off that strand of the story.

We return to the king and his empty banqueting hall. He addresses his remaining servants: 'The wedding is ready, but those invited were not worthy.' 'Worthy' is a word of which Matthew is fond, and it creeps into his retelling of the story here. We can well imagine that, when Jesus first told the story, the king would have used some blunter language. But at this point his behaviour is suddenly as astonishing as that of his 'guests' had been. He sends his messengers out into the 'streets', literally the 'places where the ways part'. At crossroads and on tracks on the way out of towns there would be peasants talking or beggars positioning themselves to advantage, like the one Jesus himself met on the way into the city of Jericho (Luke 18:35). *These* people – far beneath the social rank of the original guests, people the king scarcely needed to impress – *these* would be the ones to enjoy the waiting feast!

The servants obey, they do a 'sweep' of the area and gather in all and sundry, 'both bad and good' (another touch of Matthew's, but no doubt Jesus would have agreed). There must have been much amazed merrymaking and many stomachs fuller than they had been for as long as their owners could remember. Then comes one of those sudden extra twists that the hearers have not been looking for.

The king comes in to 'look at his guests'. One imagines him being rather startled at the motley crew and at his own idea that had brought them there. But then he notices a man who does not have a 'wedding garment'. We must assume that festal clothing was customarily issued to guests on arrival: many of those brought in off the streets would have possessed no special clothing and it sounds as if the invitation was too urgent for them to have had time to go home and get changed. The king, addressing the man as 'friend' (the same word used by the employer to the complaining day-labourer), asks him why he is not clad for the occasion when, undoubtedly, wedding garments had been available to all at the door. The man has no response to give. The servants, who have had an eventful day, now have the unpleasant task of carrying out one final order: to bind the hands and feet of the offending guest and send him to the torture chamber. That, probably, is the ugly, earthly reality that lies behind the particular wording here, of which Matthew is fond (the 'outer darkness', the place of 'weeping and gnashing of teeth', were ways of describing the ultimate punishment of the wicked). Like the servant who was wonderfully released from debt, but then tried to throttle a colleague for a few denarii, the poor man who was wonderfully wined and dined but failed to honour his host ended up in terror and agony.

The picture of a fickle, proud, vain, cruel, human king makes sense of this story, and especially of its sinister ending, in a way that interpretations that see the king as directly standing for God fail to do. It seems that this king was motivated much more by a desire for his own honour, in the marriage celebration going ahead, than by sheer altruism. Wearing the wedding garment would show that the guests were entering into the spirit of the occasion and giving respect to the king and his son. Already angered by his intended guests' grossly offensive actions, the king is in no mood to tolerate one whose casual refusal of a wedding garment makes him look very much as if he is only there for what he can eat and drink. Perhaps, indeed, the man was offering a deliberate snub: an assertion of piety, maybe, in dissociating himself from visible identification with an immoral king's luxuriant display. Still today, clothing carries remarkable symbolic power in many situations, social and religious. If the king's reaction appears petulant, childish and amazingly cruel, indeed it is. But it is just the kind of manner in which self-serving autocrats with hugely inflated egos have tended to behave from that day to this. And for Jesus' hearers, the parable offers yet another wise warning. Don't dishonour your rulers, oppressive and objectionable though they may be. Don't provoke them. You may, surprisingly, enjoy remarkable bounty from them. But if you cross them you will come to grief.

It is interesting to compare this story with that of the rebellious vineyard tenants that immediately precedes it in Matthew. In the story of the wedding banquet, those who rebel against the king's authority are not humble tenants, as in the vineyard story, but presumably the king's wealthy associates – apart, that is, from the man of the streets who didn't put on his wedding garment. This adds further sharpness to the warning. This parable suggests that it is

Israel's leaders, those who have been maintaining a truce with the authorities like Herod and Pilate appointed by Rome, who must especially beware of cherishing dreams of independence. But the humble poor should not think that they can get away with dishonouring a king, either.

Note as well that the first victims of the misguided refusal described in the story are not royalty or aristocracy but their officials – those middlemen we now recognize well as the managers of estates and keepers of accounts and collectors of rents. It is a realistic portrayal of what happens in an uprising. The figures at the pinnacle of power are rarely the first to fall, if they fall at all. They are too well defended. They are the ones history remembers, but it is their forgotten retinues who take the blows.

It is the wrath of a human king that the story depicts, but those with ears to hear would have detected again the tones of the prophet, warning, just like his predecessors, that the judgement of God himself hung over the foolish and violent. They might also have detected that quirky, characteristic edge of mysterious hope. In the midst of a harsh and alien regime a feast was spread for the poor. And they could enjoy it – if they were sufficiently humble to play by the rules, not of Yahweh's supposed representatives, but of the pagan rulers. That seems to have been the earthy, practical wisdom of Jesus in a land bubbling with tension and foreboding. It is no wonder he became so unpopular in some quarters.

The Great Banquet:
Luke 14:15–24

One of the dinner guests, on hearing this, said to him, 'Blessed is anyone who will eat bread in the kingdom of God!' Then Jesus said to him, 'Someone gave a great dinner and invited many. At the time for the dinner he sent his slave to say to those

who had been invited, "Come; for everything is ready now."
But they all alike began to make excuses. The first said to him,
"I have bought a piece of land, and I must go out and see it;
please accept my regrets." Another said, "I have bought five
yoke of oxen, and I am going to try them out; please accept my
regrets." Another said, "I have just been married, and therefore I cannot come." So the slave returned and reported this to
his master. Then the owner of the house became angry and said
to his slave, "Go out at once into the streets and lanes of the
town and bring in the poor, the crippled, the blind, and the
lame." And the slave said, "Sir, what you ordered has been
done, and there is still room." Then the master said to the
slave, "Go out into the roads and lanes, and compel people to
come in, so that my house may be filled. For I tell you, none of
those who were invited will taste my dinner." '

This banquet story told by Luke may or may not have been
originally one and the same as that found in Matthew. It is as
likely that Jesus repeated himself, with variations, on any
number of occasions as it is that the Evangelists had different
versions of the same story to hand or retold it in such a way
as to fit into their concerns – but this makes us none the
wiser. It is productive, however, to imagine the particular
overtones of the different versions as Jesus' hearers may
have listened to them in different settings.

The first thing we notice about the setting in which Luke
has placed his banquet story is that Jesus is at a meal with a
leading Pharisee. The social significance of eating together
was powerful. It was a sign that Jesus was happy to be
friends with the Pharisees, just as he was with the customs
officers. It was a token of mutual respect and honour. But
at this particular meal in Luke 14 the social codes were
directly challenged by the chief guest.

First, Jesus healed a paralysed man who appeared some-
where in the precincts. It was the Sabbath day, and Jesus

was well aware of the disapproval of his host and his other guests, but they held their tongues. Next, he pointed out how their habit of going for the best seats at dinner parties really lacked common sense. If you wanted to be honoured you were safer going to the lowest place with the hope of perhaps being asked to come higher than going to the highest and risk being asked to go down lower. Third, he dispensed some more advice that they probably did not want to hear: that they should not invite all their social equals to their parties, but the poor, weak and outcast. The reason for this would no doubt have baffled some hearers: in order *not* to be repaid! This would have run so counter to the social conventions of mutual giving of honour (as it would in many social sets today) that it would probably have remained a complete puzzle to them. There would be repayment, Jesus says, at the 'resurrection of the just' – a message that a rich man like the one who ignored the beggar at his gate would have done well to heed.

At this point another member of the party voices a conventionally pious sentiment, apparently seizing on Jesus' reference to the 'resurrection of the just' to try to establish some common ground: 'Blessed is anyone who will eat bread in the kingdom of God!' The 'feast' of God's kingdom was something eagerly expected by faithful Jews. But if the intention of the man was to divert attention away from Jesus' uncomfortable words of rebuke and advice about etiquette and hospitality by turning the conversation to the safely distant future, he did not succeed, for at this point we read that Jesus told a version of the story of the banquet. And notwithstanding the standard attempts to find 'spiritual' meanings and lessons in the story, it was surely, in its original setting, as practical, immediate and uncomfortable as the wise words that Jesus had just been uttering. What it asks the hearers to imagine is nothing less than this: that the feast of God's kingdom, for which they so piously hoped as a distant future reality, might actually come about in their own houses, at any time.

The story form so typical of Jesus both gives the hearers the necessary distance – the message is not rammed down their throats – and engages their psyche on a deeper level than a piece of 'straight' teaching or exhortation. As he tells the story in this context the emphasis seems to be rather different from the wedding banquet tale, which Matthew records as being told during Jesus' last week in Jerusalem. In the case of the wedding banquet, there was, as we saw, a warning thrust, especially to the Jewish leaders, not to play around with the fragile good will of their Gentile-appointed masters. Here the picture is more gentle and positive. The burden is not so much to warn against refusal – the worst thing that happens to the refusers, despite the anger of the host, is that they do not taste the banquet, which they apparently did not wish to do anyway. Rather, it is to picture the outrageous scene of good, decent people like Jesus' host and his friends offering hospitality to the poor and outcast of every kind. It is, in other words, a challenge to hosts, not a warning to guests.

So let us listen with these Pharisees and lawyers as the story proceeds. The host, here, is obviously 'one of them'. He is simply 'a certain man', wealthy enough to lay on a great dinner for many guests, but not a king, and it is not a wedding. Rather than sending out a party of officials to gather the assembled company at the appropriate time he sends out a single servant to do the rounds. And here Jesus starts to picture for his Pharisaic friends not acts of insolent rebelliousness, but the kind of polite excuses which, we may assume, would have been as common in that society as in ours. These guests would certainly have been regarded as rude, since they had already accepted the invitation, and their absence would indeed have angered the host, but there is no question of sending out private armies. One is busy with a new piece of land; another has bought some oxen and needs to go and try them out; another has just got married. Jesus just gives three examples, but apparently the entire guest list evaporated in this way. The excuses are very lame and the idea of being snubbed by a whole party like this would have sounded exaggerated in an amusing way. Jesus is poking fun at the fickleness of individuals even within the social set who adhered so carefully to codes of honour and shame.

The question is, what would people like Jesus' host do if this *did* happen? The host in the story had a plan. When the servant reports back the master, in anger, tells him to go out into the streets and lanes and bring in the poor, the crippled, the blind and the lame: those who were deprived of many of life's good things and left to one side in shame and social stigma. This the servant does, but still there is room. So there is one last magnificently all-inclusive invitation. The servant is to go to the 'roads and lanes', probably the by-ways outside the towns, and the fences or hedges bordering property, where beggars would skulk. He is to urge them to come in – the lowest of the low, whoever he finds. They would need almost press-ganging, for the cultural instinct would have been to refuse a sudden and unexpected invitation like this. The final word sounds as if said through gritted teeth. 'None of those who were invited will taste my dinner': 'They don't know what they're missing, but it serves them right that they're missing it!'

What would it be like if *that* were the response of an insulted host? To see in the petty excuses of one's invited guests the superficiality and tediousness of a social round that was little more than mutual back-scratching, and suddenly to break the mould, and discover what true hospitality was all about? That is the question the story would have left hanging in the air at that real-life dinner party.

Probably only a small minority of people, in that generation or any generation, have discovered by experience what
it is like. But the hint Jesus drops is this: that it is like the
feast of God's kingdom.

17

Empty Flasks

The Wise and Foolish Bridesmaids:
Matthew 25:1–12

'Then the kingdom of heaven will be like this. Ten bridesmaids took their lamps and went to meet the bridegroom. Five of them were foolish, and five were wise. When the foolish took their lamps, they took no oil with them; but the wise took flasks of oil with their lamps. As the bridegroom was delayed, all of them became drowsy and slept. But at midnight there was a shout, "Look! Here is the bridegroom! Come out to meet him." Then all those bridesmaids got up and trimmed their lamps. The foolish said to the wise, "Give us some of your oil, for our lamps are going out." But the wise replied, "No! there will not be enough for you and for us; you had better go to the dealers and buy some for yourselves." And while they went to buy it, the bridegroom came, and those who were ready went with him into the wedding banquet; and the door was shut. Later the other bridesmaids came also, saying, "Lord, lord, open to us." But he replied, "Truly I tell you, I do not know you." '

Here is another wedding scene, very different from the banquet we saw in the last chapter. We are looking at the event from the position of ten 'bridesmaids'. The function of these girls in the marriage customs of the day was obviously rather different from that familiar to us now. Many details of these customs are now lost to us, but it seems that the girls would have escorted bridegroom and bride from her home to his for the marriage feast. There were more brides-maids than at the kind of weddings people in the West are mostly familiar with now and this suggests that they were not the carefully chosen close family members or friends who tend to be 'bridesmaids' today. This is a detail that will be important at the end of the story. Both this story and that of the wedding banquet presuppose the custom that the feast took place at the bridegroom's family home. Although the focus of this story is quite different, there is an impor-tant connection. It is yet another parable with a warning edge and a way of wisdom revealed at its heart.

There is no indication of what sort of position this particular bridegroom occupied in society. He is more like the anonymous host of Luke's banquet parable than the king of Matthew's. But he, and all those involved in the cele-brations, are involved in the web of social expectations and demands like everybody else. A wedding in the West today is one of the comparatively few occasions where such social expectations are still prominent, even though the actual customs may vary widely from place to place. In Jesus' time in Palestine, written or unwritten codes dictating social behaviour and dividing the 'insider' from the 'outsider' would have applied across every area of life.

The bridesmaids may already have been assisting the bride in her preparations, but that stage in the proceedings is not mentioned. Their role now is to escort the couple in a torchlight procession. The torches may simply have been oily rags wound round sticks. Their job, therefore, was the simple one of making sure their 'lamps' were alight and ready for the procession once the bridegroom arrived. They wanted to be ready to greet him, so they 'went out' of the bride's house with lamps lit, no doubt with eager anticipation, to keep a look-out.

They could not, however, be sure of his time of arrival (that prerogative has passed to the bride in our culture!). Five of the girls had come prepared for a possible delay by bringing extra oil in a flask with them. But the other five had neglected this precaution. No doubt to begin with none of them thought this would matter: surely he would be here soon.

Unfortunately, that is not what happened. The scene is comical. The torches remained alight but the bridegroom was so long in coming that the girls all dozed off to sleep. Perhaps Jesus had been at a wedding like this, maybe as one of the guests in the bridegroom's house, with the feast waiting to be eaten while the bridegroom unaccountably had not arrived. Perhaps the bridegroom was out partying with his male friends (a custom also not unknown today). It is like picturing a contemporary wedding where the bride is so delayed that the congregation start to nod off in the pews.

Then, at midnight, somebody cries out. Perhaps a sound has stirred one of the girls; perhaps it is somebody inside the house – maybe the anxious bride herself. 'He's coming! Come on, let's meet him!' The groom and his friends have been spotted some way down the road. The bridesmaids stumble blearily to their feet. They attend to their lamps, pulling away the bits of rag that are now parched and crumbling, finding clean parts to douse with oil so that there will be bright flames for the procession. But now the prudence of the one group and the carelessness of the other have their respective payoffs. Those with no extra oil have nothing with which to rekindle the flame. They ask the others for some of their oil, but the prudent girls respond that there might not be enough to go round. Better (the implication is) that some lamps should be properly lit in a way that will last the distance of the walk than that they should share it round and risk any or all of the lamps going out on the procession! So their advice to the others is to go and buy some oil. This sounds surprising at midnight (before the days, probably, of 'eight till late'!). Perhaps what the prudent girls had in mind was that they should go and wake a sleeping shopkeeper – a rather similar picture to one Jesus uses elsewhere (Luke 11:5–8). Our idea of 'shops' is in any case rather anachronistic. Many people, not least those with a little piece of land, might have sold commodities such as olive oil.

But wherever they went to get their oil it took too long. Soon the bridegroom had arrived at the bride's house. The procession was underway with only half the planned number of torchbearers. They had reached the bridegroom's house before the other girls had returned. The party went in to the waiting banquet and the door was shut. It was, after all, night-time, and intruders and suspicious gatecrashers were not wanted.

Then the other five bridesmaids returned, whether with oil or not, we do not know, and in any case it was too late to make any difference. They come and knock and plead to be let in. But they receive a curt response from inside. The bridegroom says 'I don't know you', with the implication, why should I open my door to strangers at this time of night?

Could the other bridesmaids not have told the bridegroom who these late callers were? Surely they would not be so heartless as to let their friends be kept outside? Perhaps they did tell him. Perhaps the bridegroom might subsequently have had pity on them and let them in. But that is to go beyond the story. The picture we are left with is sad and stark. Five girls, who have been gearing up for the event of the year, have missed not only playing their special part but also the climax of the evening: the wedding banquet. And that is the real unhappiness for them. Making a fool of themselves by not having enough oil for the procession might have been forgotten in the fun and feasting of the wedding supper. But at the end they were left out completely, dark, cold and lonely.

Weighty, sombre theological meanings have become attached to this story, as to the others: we shall explore some briefly in Chapter 19. But it is important, once more, to see this first as a three-dimensional story reflecting a realistic situation in Jesus' social world. That means we should hear the lightness of touch in Jesus' voice. Those who are careless about fulfilling their role in an important social event may well find that they are excluded from the fun of it. The notion of a total or permanent exclusion from happiness would have made no sense in the context of the situation being pictured. It is simply that the girls' big night ends up – or *might* end up – in tears of disappointment.

There is a parallel here with the mood of Luke's banquet story: the excuse makers are foolish, though they do not realize it. These girls are foolish, and, by implication, they do come to realize it. All are excluded from the banquet. The contrast between wisdom and folly is one that runs through the Bible and is prominent in the teaching of Jesus.

The story connects with the great theme of celebration that runs through the Gospel narratives. Jesus was accused on account of being a party-goer. But in his eyes his socializing was the start of God's kingdom party. Some were too superior and suspicious to join in; these girls in the story were simply unprepared. But the result for both them, eagerly awaiting the party, and the likes of the Pharisees, looking askance at it, would be the same: exclusion. Their tale is a warning not just to 'prepare for God's kingdom' in a vague or spiritualized sense but carefully to fulfil responsibilities in the social settings (with all their compromises) in which, surprisingly, God's kingdom is to be found.

18

Playing Safe

The Talents:
Matthew 25:14–30

'For it is as if a man, going on a journey, summoned his slaves and entrusted his property to them; to one he gave five talents, to another two, to another one, to each according to his ability. Then he went away. The one who had received the five talents went off at once and traded with them, and made five more talents. In the same way, the one who had the two talents made two more talents. But the one who had received the one talent went off and dug a hole in the ground and hid his master's money. After a long time the master of those slaves came and settled accounts with them. Then the one who had received the five talents came forward, bringing five more talents, saying, "Master, you handed over to me five talents; see, I have made five more talents." His master said to him, "Well done, good and trustworthy slave; you have been trustworthy in a few things, I will put you in charge of many things; enter into the joy of your master." And the one with the two talents also came forward, saying, "Master, you handed over to me two talents; see, I have made two more talents." His master said to him, "Well done, good and trustworthy slave; you have been trustworthy in a few things, I will put you in charge of many things; enter into the joy of your master." Then the one who had received the one talent also came forward, saying, "Master, I knew that you were a harsh man, reaping where you did not sow, and gathering where you did not scatter seed; so I was afraid, and I went and hid your talent in the ground. Here you have what is yours." But his master replied, "You wicked and lazy slave! You knew, did you, that I reap where I did not sow, and gather where I did not scatter? Then you ought to have invested my money with the bankers, and on my return I would have received what was my own with interest. So take the talent from him, and give it to the one with the ten talents. For to all those who have, more will be given, and they will have an abundance; but from those who have nothing, even what they have will be taken away. As for this worthless slave, throw him into the outer darkness, where there will be weeping and gnashing of teeth." '

For those who had plenty of money the strategies and instincts of investment and trade were as vibrant in Jesus' culture as they are in our own. Riches bring with them the power to make more riches. This is first of all a story about the handling of money. 'Talent' has come into English as a word meaning 'ability' or 'skill', but we should put that idea aside as we come to the tale, and realize instead that a 'talent' was a large sum of money. To give modern equivalents is always hazardous but it is reckoned that a day-labourer like those engaged at grape harvest would need to work all the year round for fifteen years to earn a *single* talent.

The man is therefore one of the very wealthy élite. Like the vineyard owner with the rebellious tenants, this man is also a traveller, perhaps owning estates abroad as well. The particular journey he goes on here necessitates, it seems, a considerable delegation of power to his 'bondservants', those highly respected and trustworthy members of the 'slave' class, of whom we have already met a number. For whatever reason, he would not have personal opportunity in the immediate future to make important business decisions, so he hands over to three of his most trusted subordinates very large sums, varying according to their 'ability' – presumably the adroitness at playing the markets that he perceived in them. It would have been a pity to entrust a lesser sum to a shrewd operator with the capacity to make a one hundred per cent gain on it; equally, it would have been a risk to entrust a larger sum to a less capable financier who might make a loss. So one slave receives five talents, one two, and one just a single talent.

The two more 'able' slaves do their boss proud. Immediately they start trading and double the capital they have received. The third slave, however, has a different approach. For reasons that will start to become clear later he seems not to find the idea of trading either attractive or wise. He simply digs a hole in the ground and hides the money.

In due course, after a long absence, the owner of the money returns. Naturally, he wants to see what growth has been achieved, so he summons his agents. The first makes his little speech, presenting the fruit of his efforts. The master praises him in words that carry the characteristic flavour of Matthew's Gospel: he is a 'good and faithful servant'. He has been 'faithful' over a few things – the servant might not have reckoned five talents to be 'few', but still! – and his reward will be a still higher degree of responsibility: 'I will set you over many things'. Initially, perhaps, this simply means that he is now charged with taking the *ten* talents into the market. The master's closing words, 'Enter into the joy of your master', sound loftily theological and seem to reflect the 'divine' meaning that was put upon the story from early times. In the context of the realistic setting that Jesus is portraying, a more down-to-earth, backslapping plaudit can be imagined. The point is that the slave, through proving his ability, has secured a highly favoured place in the master's esteem, like the manager in another story who surprisingly wins such a place by reducing the debts of some of his master's clients.

The scene repeats itself precisely with the second slave, who shows the owner the two talents he has made. The owner gives him exactly the same words of approval. But then it is the turn of the third servant.

One assumes that this servant was well aware of the exploits of his colleagues. He may also have been present at the audience at which they had just reported their achievement, or have seen the glow on their faces as they left. But whether he would have felt apprehension as his turn to be interviewed approached is an interesting question. He has his own reasons ready to hand for the way he has handled the master's money, and is perhaps confident that they will be accepted on their merits.

These reasons are, in their way, good ones. He knows the master to be a 'hard man'. The expansion he gives of this description fits closely with what we know of ancient landowning aristocracies, such as those that held sway in first-century Palestine, as well as with what we know of the behaviour of ruthless and greedy men in every generation. He 'reaps where he did not sow, and gathers where he did not scatter'. He is representative of the landlords who gradually, through rents and taxes, accumulated the land of the peasants. Their poverty now funds his luxury. Knowing this, the servant, as he honestly admits, was afraid, and so went and hid the talent with which he was entrusted. Anxious lest he should lose something belonging to so harsh a master, his one thought was to preserve it intact. And so, with an air perhaps of obsequious self-satisfaction, he dusts off the bag of gold and hands it over.

The owner is not impressed. Calling the servant 'wicked and lazy' he points out to him that the logic of his argument should have led him in the exact opposite direction. Knowing that the master 'reaped where he did not sow, and

gathered where he did not scatter' – a description the master
is apparently quite happy with! – he should have imitated
some of the master's approach and tried to get something
for nothing. He could have done this easily enough just by
taking the money to some bankers who would, in due
course, have returned it with interest. He did not need the
energy or astuteness of the other traders for that. As it is, he
has proved his unfitness for further responsibility of this
kind. So the newly exhumed talent must be entrusted to the
servant with the ten talents who has more than proved his
worth. The master backs this decision up with a piece of
standard capitalist wisdom: 'To all those who have, more
will be given, and they will have an abundance; but from
those who have nothing, even what they have will be taken
away.' It is seen to apply to the possession not only of
wealth but also of positions of responsibility (which are, of
course, in themselves 'wealth' of a different kind). The landowner and others like him are in a very strong position to
make themselves ever wealthier; those at the bottom of the
social pile are very vulnerable to the descent to absolute
poverty, beggary and death. Retainers of the rich who play
the rich men's game may not, indeed, *possess* riches as a
result, but they will enhance their status and security. Those
who do not play along will find that they lose what status
and security they had.

There is a still worse fate, though, for the third servant
than losing the privilege of being one of his master's trading
agents. Like the man who refused to don a wedding
garment, snubbing the spirit of ostentatious festivity, he is
to be thrown (presumably by his fellow servants) 'into the
outer darkness, where there will be weeping and gnashing
of teeth'. The language is coloured by beliefs about ultimate
punishment; but its origin, and its unpleasant meaning in
the context of the story, is once again the torture chamber.
Such places existed then, as they still do.

So a familiar warning emerges through another vivid portrayal of an aspect of Palestinian life. Go along with your
overlords, and it will go well with you. Go against them,
and it will go ill. Not only is the paralysing fear of the
third servant, which led him so to misjudge his way, a dire
warning. The activity of the other two, embracing fully
the money-making enterprise of their master, is one of
Jesus' most surprising examples. The implication is clear.
The day for Pharisaic scruples about involvement in the
muddy waters of Gentile finance is over. Lending money at
interest may be a wise course of action; even bolder market
transactions may be better still. And this not because the
capitalist-type system is good, or oppression is right, or the
master is just, but because shielding oneself from the affairs
of the world in an attempt to preserve purity is not the way
either to personal holiness or national security. This was
the paradoxical, sombre and provocative message of Jesus
to his contemporaries. They would only be saved by God as
a holy and victorious people through surrender to the
authority of their pagan rulers. In Matthew's story of
Jesus' life this tale comes very shortly before Jesus himself
would lead the way and be handed over to the Romans to
be executed.

The Pounds:
Luke 19:11–27

As they were listening to this, he went on to tell a parable,
because he was near Jerusalem, and because they supposed
that the kingdom of God was to appear immediately. So he
said, 'A nobleman went to a distant country to get royal power
for himself and then return. He summoned ten of his slaves,
and gave them ten pounds, and said to them, "Do business
with these until I come back." But the citizens of his country

hated him and sent a delegation after him, saying, "We do not want this man to rule over us." When he returned, having received royal power, he ordered these slaves, to whom he had given the money, to be summoned so that he might find out what they had gained by trading. The first came forward and said, "Lord, your pound has made ten more pounds." He said to him, "Well done, good slave! Because you have been trustworthy in a very small thing, take charge of ten cities." Then the second came, saying, "Lord, your pound has made five pounds." He said to him, "And you, rule over five cities." Then the other came, saying, "Lord, here is your pound. I wrapped it up in a piece of cloth, for I was afraid of you, because you are a harsh man; you take what you did not deposit, and reap what you did not sow." He said to him, "I will judge you by your own words, you wicked slave! You knew, did you, that I was a harsh man, taking what I did not deposit and reaping what I did not sow? Why then did you not put my money into the bank? Then when I returned, I could have collected it with interest." He said to the bystanders, "Take the pound from him and give it to the one who has ten pounds." (And they said to him, "Lord, he has ten pounds!") "I tell you, to all those who have, more will be given; but from those who have nothing, even what they have will be taken away. But as for these enemies of mine who did not want me to be king over them – bring them here and slaughter them in my presence." '

The undercurrents of rebellion or conformity that we have detected in Matthew's version of the story of the slaves entrusted with money to trade with are seen on the surface in Luke's. Both versions are set by the Evangelists in contexts of warning: Matthew in his last 'discourse' of Jesus just days before the crucifixion; Luke a little earlier in the narrative, just before Jesus enters Jerusalem for the last time. Luke suggests that Jesus told the story because his approach to

Jerusalem, followed by crowds, was arousing increasingly feverish expectation that God was about to act decisively to bring in his kingdom. In the crowd's mind this probably meant that Jesus was to be at the head of a successful uprising against the Roman authorities and their compliant Jewish associates.

The parable is generally taken in this context as Jesus' way of dampening down speculation by pointing to the fact that, like the 'nobleman', he himself needed to go into a 'far country' before receiving his kingdom. However, this is the kind of 'spiritualization' of a parable that we shall discuss in the next chapter. It seems as if the immediate identification of Jesus with the king has led most interpreters off on a false trail – not 'false' in the sense that the resonances of this spiritual meaning are not valuable to explore, but in the sense that it almost certainly obscures the original thrust of the parable as a coherent, realistic story.

We will understand the story much more closely as its first hearers would have understood it and see its clear appropriateness to the setting Luke gives it if we follow the pattern we have seen in the other stories. That is, the 'nobleman' would probably have been neither heard nor intended as a reference to Jesus. He is, rather, a realistic representative of the aristocracy, a man of noble blood, indeed, with royal connections and destiny. He takes up the mantle of kingship and brooks no adversaries. So the story warns Jesus' hearers not by suggesting that 'Jesus must go away before he can be king', but by reminding them of what human kings do to rebels, and perhaps of what one king in particular did. In the starkest fashion Jesus was steering the crowds away from any idea that the kingdom of God and the rescue of Israel was about to come through a rebellion against Rome. If that was the crowd's intention – latching on to Jesus as a figurehead – they would soon find that it would lead not to victory and vindication but to merciless slaughter. As things would turn out, the message was not heeded. This crowd escaped in the short term, but Jesus was slaughtered on the altar of their misconception of God's kingdom. The populace of Jerusalem some forty years later, still not having heeded Jesus' message of non-violence and submission, suffered terrible destruction at the hands of the Romans.

So the nobleman went into a 'far country'. More specific than Matthew's man 'going on a journey', this phrase echoes exactly the destination of the prodigal son. In addition, it echoes an event that had taken place in 4 BCE when Archelaus, a son of Herod the Great, had gone to Rome to receive the official imprimatur of kingship. The picture conjures up the scenario of rule by the Gentile-dominated aristocracy with which we have now become very familiar. These are the people of the 'far country', bringing defilement upon Israel's holy land, ruling oppressively over her holy nation. They are the people of whom many in that holy land and nation want to be rid.

Like the man in Matthew's version this aristocrat summons his senior 'slaves' and commissions them to carry on with his financial dealings while he is away. In this case, however, less is made of this arrangement. No distinction is drawn between the capabilities of the different officials. The money is counted in 'minas' or 'pounds', a much smaller amount than a talent, worth one hundred denarii. We hear simply of ten servants entrusted with ten pounds, apparently one each, and the hearers are left at this point simply to assume that they traded with them as they were instructed. The climax of this part of the story, however, is the action of the subjects-to-be of the new king. They send a special party after him to plead with the Roman authorities not to appoint him as king. This too echoes the historical record regarding Archelaus, who even before he was king was intensely disliked for his cruelty, and was followed to Rome by a deputation pleading (unsuccessfully) for his appointment to be revoked.

The hearers are in suspense, knowing the outcome of the historical event, but waiting to see how Jesus' story will turn out. The newly confirmed king returns and attention focuses back on to the traders. He summons them to see how successful they have been. Although ten were originally mentioned, only three appear at this point: as with Matthew's version, the important thing is the contrast between the active traders and the passive hoarder, not any distinctions among the active traders. The first comes to report that his pound has made a profit not of a mere hundred per cent but of a thousand! The master's words of commendation are similar to those in Matthew's story, but there is no mention of the 'joy' of the master – there is a more realistic emphasis on the actual meaning of the new responsibility with which the slave is entrusted. He is to have 'authority' over ten cities, no doubt in administering the king's affairs, probably in the financial realm especially, with the supervision of rent collection, tax collection and the like. The second slave has made a five hundred per cent profit on his pound, but the master's response is quickly passed over by the storyteller ('Great – you look after five cities') as we hasten to the tale of the third servant.

In Luke's version we have no idea up to this point that any of the slaves has done anything other than trade with the money as instructed. It comes as a shock to the hearers, therefore, to hear the unctuous tones of the third servant. 'Master, here is your pound [singular!] which I kept wrapped up in a cloth.' This was not the careful burial carried out by the third slave in the other story but a piece of rather careless money minding. The hearers would already foresee what was going to happen. The excuse is as in Matthew: 'I was afraid of you, because you are a hard man;

you take what you did not deposit, and reap what you did not sow.' 'You take what you did not deposit' is a more pointed expression than Matthew's 'you gather where you did not scatter'. It plainly evokes the forcible expropriation of others' wealth.

The master's response is very similar to that in the other story, except that instead of calling the servant 'wicked' and 'lazy', he is content with 'wicked'. The servant's 'own mouth' has condemned him. If he knew that his lord was grasping and acquisitive he should have tried to make his money grow. The bystanders – other officials – are told to remove the one pound from this servant and hand it over to the successful servant who made ten pounds from one. The officials make a token protest, but the master gives the good capitalist answer: 'To every one who has ...'. There is no room in this economy for the one who will not pull their weight.

That, however, is the end of the matter as far as the third servant is concerned: no further punishment is meted out other than this stripping of responsibility. But the climax of the story is still to come. What of the embassy to Rome petitioning against the king's rule? They had obviously not succeeded. Unfortunately, the king had got wind of it. Those behind the idea were still there; perhaps the ambassadors themselves had now returned. Any who might have tried to conceal their part in the plot might well have been betrayed by those anxious to keep on the new king's side. The king commands that his enemies be brought, and – in a touch of pride and symbolic brutality very characteristic of Roman regimes – slaughtered *in his presence*.

Here, then, is yet another variation on the now-familiar theme. A story is told which graphically warns against arousing the hostility of an already harsh governing class. Do not think, Jesus says, that the kingdom of God and the renewal of Israel that goes along with it is going to come 'immediately' through rebelling against your godless rulers. Do not even think it is going to come by trying to keep your hands clean from their aggressive trading practices. That way lies only defeat and destruction. But if it *is* coming – as Jesus said it was – *how* will it come? This is where, perhaps, our account of Jesus' tales must come full circle. The kingdom comes not through violence or through anxious protection from the defilement of the pagan world. It comes rather with the mystery, the naturalness, the silence and the certainty of the seed that finds good soil despite all odds, and grows to a harvest.

19

Tellings of the Tales

The assumption we have been making throughout this book is that the stories of Jesus have an inner coherence and logic that enable us to imagine the kind of resonance and effect they would have had for those who first heard them. They seem to reflect in considerable detail the world in which Jesus actually lived. Through the subtle and provocative means of narrative, Jesus was urging people to think differently about that world, to discern where and how the hand of God was truly at work, and behave differently as a result.

Before we draw together in our final chapter the threads of the various stories, so as to draw up a profile of their teller and his message, it is important to look here at the way in which the understanding and use of the parables changed and developed over time. For the account of the probable original thrust of the tales that I have offered in this book is by no means the normal interpretation of them. From very early times a rich variety of deeper or 'spiritual' meanings was seen in the parables. That tradition has continued to this day, even among scholars who claim to have left it behind! This was a natural process. For the first millennium and a half of Christian history the stories *about* Jesus and the stories *of* Jesus were passed on in a predominantly oral manner. Manuscripts, and even printed books in the early days of printing, were for the minority. Oral communication

can awaken all sorts of echoes and suggest all sorts of corre-
spondences that the fixity of the written or printed word
may seem to limit. Of course, the stories were also handed
on in written form in the Bible, and that also contributed
to the process of development of their meanings; for they
jostled alongside many other richly suggestive texts, whose
mutual conjunction prompted imaginative interpretative
links in the minds of those who could read and teach. All
in all the parables, with their vivid imagery, were seen as
superb preaching tools when used to elucidate the range
of Christian doctrines and to convey the comforts and
warnings of the Christian gospel.

In this process, naturally, the original force of the parables
on the lips of Jesus and in the minds of his hearers got
blunted and often almost forgotten. With our knowledge
of the history and society of first-century Palestine it is, I
believe, possible to feel that original force again quite
sharply. But this does not mean that we lay aside the long
tradition of interpretation as simply misguided (though
some aspects of it should, as we shall see, be rejected on
moral grounds). Often it has yielded a wealth of imaginative reflection on the stories, which, though it may not take
us to the sense and power of the parables for Jesus and his
hearers, does give us fine fare for meditation on the larger
meaning and implications of Jesus' coming in history. So
today we have the opportunity to learn not only from a
historically informed study of the parables such as I have
tried to pursue in this book but also from the many-sided
tellings of the tales down the centuries.

Let us then trace in outline, with some examples, four
intertwined ways in which the meaning of the parables has
become 'enriched' over the centuries.

First, there has been development of the echoes of the Old
Testament Scriptures that are present in the stories. We

have seen that, as a part of the original story, some such echoes would already have been important for Jesus and his hearers, though not to the detriment of the realism of the story. The vineyard, for instance, was a familiar image representing Israel, so a tale of violence in an actual vineyard would probably have evoked the prophet's condemnation of the bloodshed in Israel, the Lord's 'vineyard' (Isaiah 5:7). But the image became developed to the extent that the standard interpretation of the parable now sees the vineyard owner as representing God and the various emissaries his prophets, and of course his son, Jesus. It is interesting to observe the number of commentators who assume that this was the way that Matthew, Mark and Luke themselves understood the parable, as if already the more immediate, realistic meaning had been lost. There are hints, as we shall see below, that certainly suggest that they heard resonances like this; and yet they preserve the realistic story with its clear warning of the consequences of violent uprising in which the vineyard owner is a thoroughly human type. It is subsequent commentators who are responsible for the full-blown development of the meaning.

Another very familiar image was that of the banquet or wedding festival. The hope of a new age of bliss was described in terms of a feast (Isaiah 25:6). So the 'kingdom of God' to which people looked forward eagerly, and whose arrival Jesus announced, was a new era of celebration, and there are strong overtones of this in the banquet parables as well as that of the bridesmaids. When Jesus told these stories, there would, as we have seen, have been an immediate social implication in the setting of his hearers, that it was foolish to stand aloof or treat carelessly the celebrations going on around them – even though (or especially when!) they were the revelries of an impious king. Jesus himself is recorded as enacting his message through his sharing of meals with all types of people, including those regarded by the pious as off limits. But, in time, this imagery of feasting came to suggest less the actual social embodiment of God's kingdom and more 'the church' in general terms as the bearer of the kingdom. So God was seen as the host inviting guests to his feast: when the privileged guests (often interpreted as the Jewish race) refused, others (the Gentiles) were brought in. (The phrase 'compel them to come in' – right enough for an arrogant host who has been jilted of his honour, dealing with naturally bewildered invitees – was even used, most unfortunately, to justify the forcible 'conversion' of peoples by Christian missionaries.)

There are many other echoes of the Old Testament Scriptures in the parables. These place the stories firmly in the stream of Jewish tradition and prompt interesting comparisons and reflections. For instance, the story of the prodigal son has many similarities with Old Testament stories of a father and two sons. It is impossible to say to what extent such comparisons and echoes were in the mind of Jesus and his first hearers. But we have seen that, in every case, the stories offer a vignette of Jesus' own world, which makes sense on its own terms. It is natural that the significance of the echoes has seemed to grow as people have had time to ponder them. But it is a shame if that significance is allowed to obscure completely an original realistic scene that carries its own highly suggestive evocations.

Second, and closely connected to the first point, the Evangelists in their rendering of the stories have sometimes used language that directly breaks into the realistic scene with sombre theological terminology. The clearest examples of this are in the gospel of Matthew, and we have noted them already. The man without a wedding garment and the hoarder who should have been a trader are to be 'thrown into the outer darkness, where there is wailing and gnashing of teeth'. This is the language of ultimate punishment and it

sits ill with the realism of the stories up to that point. This
is not necessarily to say that Jesus never spoke the language
of ultimate punishment, but the stories (and other things
he said) strongly suggest that the defining crisis for his
people lay in the immediate, not the far distant, future. The
language of darkness and anguish is brought into conjunction with the stories as a way of reinforcing, after the event,
the dreadful finality for Israel of the judgement suffered after
failing to heed the warnings of Jesus. There is also the positive and exalted phraseology of the rich man's address to his
two successful traders: 'enter into the joy of your master'.

These examples show an almost irresistible tendency to
start identifying the master and father figures of the parables
directly with God himself, seen as the one who commands,
forgives, rewards and punishes. This is problematic in so
far as it tends to block from view the very clearly human
qualities of these figures, and so causes us to miss much of
the actual storyline of a parable and its social resonance.
Whether it is the vulnerability of the prodigal's father, or
the fickleness of the king who forgives then tortures, or the
harshness of the magnate who reaps where he has not sown
and gathers where he has not scattered, the force of the
narratives will be dissipated if we bypass their humanness. Conversely, it is precisely embarrassment about the
all-too-human appearance of many of these characters
that has caused many readers to minimize the importance
of a parable's details on the grounds that God cannot
possibly be compared to such a person. It is said that
Jesus simply used such homely tales as a way of getting a
point across to people. But this view ends up being self-
contradictory, as if Jesus used vivid homely tales to speak
about God, but really wanted people to forget most of the
details because they were misleading! It seems to me that it
is much more likely that he intended no equation of these
figures with God in the first place.

But the process of turning these into 'God' stories, of which we can see the first signs in the Gospels themselves, may have happened quite naturally as the outworking of the belief that God was at work in the events of history and especially in the judgement and blessing of his people. So the story of the judge and the widow is closely linked to the assurance that 'God will vindicate his elect'. This does not mean that either Jesus or Luke saw the judge as a direct representation of God, but it does suggest that in events such as the vindication of a helpless widow by a profane judge God himself was exercising his sovereign rule. Conversely, the consigning of a forgiven but grasping slave to the torture chamber would not have been seen as a direct representation of the way God treats a forgiven but unforgiving person, notwithstanding the verse 'So also my heavenly Father will do to every one of you ...'. But in events such as the treatment meted out by a changeable human king to a foolish retainer who does not see which way the wind is blowing, God also was exercising his sovereign rule. That was probably left implicit by Jesus for his hearers; the language in which the Gospel writers record the stories and associated sayings makes it explicit. Later developments that saw these stories as literal pictures of divine punishment are to be regretted.

The most famous and striking figure of the parables to have been seen as a representation of God is the father of the prodigal son. Given Jesus' encouragement to his disciples to address God as 'Father' (Matthew 6:9; Luke 11:2) and his description of God as merciful and generous (Matthew 5:45; Luke 6:35–6) this was and is a natural identification to make. But again it is better to see it as a wonderful echo rather than to read the story as mere window dressing for 'spiritual' truth. God's merciful kingdom is certainly discerned behind the attitude and action of a man such as this, just as his awesome judgements are discerned behind the images of punishment meted out by ruthless human rulers. But if we rightly draw back from seeing the latter as directly literal portrayals of how God may deal with wickedness and folly, we should equally draw back from seeing the former as a directly literal portrayal of how he may have mercy on those who acknowledge their guilt and return to him. In both cases we lose out if we fail to imagine the human situation that is the story's focus.

Third, it was very natural that the parables should soon have come to be read as reflecting in some way the story of Jesus himself and the Christian understanding of his coming. Again, we find traces of such reading in the Gospel accounts themselves. It is likely, for example, that Matthew saw the 'bridegroom' in the story of the bridesmaids as an image of the Christ who would come in final judgement. Jesus had used the image in an oblique way about himself on another occasion (Matthew 9:15). The clearest instance of such a trace is in the story of the rebellious tenants. That Mark, at any rate, saw the resonance of the story with that of Jesus himself, as the Father's son coming to the vineyard Israel to collect its 'fruit', seems clear from the phrase 'beloved son' that he uses. This is the phrase that was used of Jesus at his baptism (Mark 1:11) and transfiguration (Mark 9:7). It is interesting that both Matthew and Luke drop the 'beloved'. Perhaps they felt that it drew too much attention to the parallel in an anachronistic way. Matthew and Luke, however, add their own touches: they both have the son being thrown out of the vineyard *before* being killed, generally taken as an allusion to Jesus' crucifixion outside the city. All three also use the Old Testament quotation about the rejected stone following the parable: this was often used in the early church to refer to the rejected but exalted Jesus. As we saw, it does not need to refer to him in the original setting of the story: it may simply have referred to the great reversal of fortunes and expectations as judgement fell upon Israel and her pagan enemies were allowed the upper hand.

The Evangelists' presentation of this story, however, is very restrained and easily suggests its original character as the warning tale we have described. But subsequent commentators down to the present have been very ready to see it as a full-blown representation of the story of salvation. The picture of the vulnerable murdered son – like that of the vulnerable, compassionate father in the story of the prodigal – is irresistibly evocative.

Other stories too have been seen as depictions of the drama of God's coming in Christ. Most famously, the Samaritan became interpreted as Jesus, 'coming down' from (the heavenly) Jerusalem to rescue fallen humanity, victim of the devil and his angels. The fact that sometimes the tiniest details were fitted into this schema (the 'two pence' left by the Samaritan for the innkeeper, for instance, being seen as the two sacraments of baptism and Holy Communion!) should not allow us to miss the power of such a perception of Christian truth as delineated in the contours of the story. Nor was this interpretation divorced from the strong challenge to behaviour inherent in the story: Christ was not only the neighbour who saved us, he was the model for true neighbourliness. But, again, the human resonances of the original story could easily get forgotten when such a picture took over.

If Christ is seen at the heart of the parables, elements of the stories easily become interpreted as phases or aspects of the great plan of salvation. So the day-labourers hired at different times for work in the vineyard become representative of the different historical eras in which God has called people into his kingdom, or the different stages of human life at which people enter it. A particular and often problematic emphasis in the history of interpretation has been on the respective places of the Jews and the Gentiles in God's purpose. Too often the parables have been read in a crude and wooden way as implying that the Jews as a race were simply rejected by God, following the crucifixion of Jesus, and that the Gentiles replaced them in the purpose of God. One can see how certain verses in the Gospels could give rise to this misconception. The saying that appears in Matthew at the end of the story of the rebellious tenants, 'The kingdom of God will be taken away from you and given to a nation producing the fruits of it' (Matthew 21:43), is such a one. But the fact that the word 'nation' (singular) is used warns us against seeing too hard a 'replacement' theology in this verse. It is not a question of one human nation being replaced by other nations. The emphasis is not on race but on Matthew's characteristic theme of 'fruitfulness'. The kingdom of God will belong to the obedient, whatever their race – including obedient Jews.

Unfortunately, though, this and other tales could be used in a much harsher way as reinforcing the Jew–Gentile distinction in the purposes of God. The Jews (*en masse*) were seen as those who refused the invitation to the banquet; the Gentiles as those brought in off the streets. The Jews were seen as the elder brother in his self-righteousness; the Gentiles as the younger, defiled but repentant, and therefore welcomed back into the family. The priest and Levite represented the Jewish law, unable to do any good; the Samaritan represented the way of Christ.

One can readily see how such interpretations arose. For, as we have seen, there is the strong hint in the stories that the way of wisdom and peace for Jesus' Jewish hearers is not the isolationist self-protection to which they were inclined, but a paradoxical readiness to embrace the very contact with Gentiles that many strove to avoid. When interpreters have turned these narrative hints, given at a particular juncture in history, into a fixed scheme, whereby the chosen people Israel have become the *rejected* people Israel, they have not only left the original stories behind. They have given them a malign twist, which is far removed from their true spirit.

The fact that the resonances of later Christian teaching in the tales are just that – resonances, not exact schemes to be decoded, nor the object of Jesus' original storytelling – is seen most clearly in the difficulty interpreters have had with fitting both God the Father and God the Son into the parables. On the one hand, in Matthew's version of the banquet parable, the king could of course be seen as God the Father, and the son being 'married' as Jesus Christ, the 'bridegroom' of the church. The story of the mutinous tenants also offers a neat place for both Father and Son. On the other hand, a 'king' such as the one who forgave a massive debt, or a rich man who entrusted his wealth to his servants to trade with, might be seen as God, or as Christ, or as God-in-Christ, but it is very difficult to press such stories into complete representations of the sweep of the Christian narrative. Especially, it has been notoriously hard to find a place for Father and Son together in the story of the prodigal son. The father evokes the compassionate love of God the Father. He also evokes the compassionate love of God the Son, incarnate in Jesus, welcoming and sharing meals with the defiled and the desperate. But without doing violence to the story we cannot read it as a complete pictorial account of the epic drama of God sending his Son to atone for sin and rescue the human race. That is one of the clearest indications that, originally, it was a story intended to evoke a human situation, which would enable Jesus' hearers to see their lives and his own activity with new eyes.

Fourth, the various figures in the parables have been seen in multiple ways as standing for individuals or groups in different spiritual conditions, in whatever period the interpreter is living. The main cue for such an understanding has been the interpretations given in the Gospels to the parables of the sower and of the wheat and the darnel. As we have seen, the seed sown on various kinds of soil is seen as representing the variety of responses to the word of God, whether in the ministry of Jesus, or in the early church, or at any time in Christian history. The field where wheat and darnel grow together is seen as the world in which the 'sons of the kingdom' and the 'sons of the evil one' grow alongside each other. But any of the stories are amenable to such treatment. The prodigal son is seen as the quintessential example of a repentant sinner; the Samaritan is seen as the model of care and compassion; the unforgiving servant is seen as a terrible warning to grudge-bearing Christians.

Sometimes identifications have been quite specific. The negative characters, such as the rich man who did nothing for Lazarus, have been seen as vivid reflections of those the interpreter regards as heretics or enemies of the church. Conversely, the characters who end up 'on top' have often (conveniently) been seen as images of 'us', the complacent interpreters. So the parable of the Pharisee and the tax collector fails to sting any more because Christian readers 'know' that 'we' are not like the self-righteous Pharisee! The identification of parable characters with contemporary groups can become so stereotyped that the parables become transformed from being instruments of subversion and provocation to being instruments reinforcing the self-assurance of an 'in group' and the status quo.

It is possible, however, to continue the tactic of linking parable characters with contemporary groups in such a way as to revive the shocking element of the story. This continues to be an effective tactic of preachers and Christian dramatists seeking to let the story live afresh. The Good Samaritan was turned, for instance, in the 1980s into the parable of the Good Punk Rocker by the Riding Lights Theatre Company.

Such specific retellings themselves, of course, quickly lose their novelty value. Yet the possibility always remains of transposing the stories into contemporary dress to great effect in ever new ways, in that human societies in each generation (not least the church) have their blind spots, prejudices and unwarranted preconceptions. And narrative remains a powerful means of prising minds open to new ways of thinking, and suggesting alternative visions of the world.

For such transpositions to carry the authentic power of the story, however, it should go without saying that we should constantly return to the original. And that is what we shall do in our final chapter.

20

The Profile of the Teller

So we return to the stories that have formed the subject of this book. What are the threads and themes and tell-tale touches running through them that may allow us to draw a profile of the one who told them?

I have tried to give a coherent account of these stories, showing how they best make sense on their own terms against the background of first-century Palestinian society, without presupposing that they bear various deeper 'spiritual' or doctrinal meanings. As we saw in the previous chapter, such deeper interpretations arose quite naturally before long, but also entail many mutual contradictions and the obscuring of aspects of the stories in order to make their point. Although it is safe to assume that images such as the vineyard and the banquet would in the original telling have evoked passages and themes from Israel's Scriptures, which would have been significant in the understanding of the parable, my assumption has been that the tales in each case draw their essential logic from a current social situation, not from an existing system of symbols or metaphors. The force they originally carried, and were intended to carry, seems to have lain in the oblique and needling challenge they offered to tendencies among Jesus' contemporaries in Judaism. They appear to have been imaginative invitations, drawn from very familiar scenes, to a new vision of the world, and in particular the immediate circumstances in which they found themselves. I believe that we will only understand them when we repay the compliment with a similar act of imagination that seeks to re-enter the live encounters in which they were first heard.

A word of caution is in order here. The account I have given of these parables is a result of one person's act of imagination and is offered as a way of drawing them together in a consistent pattern. I have spoken of the parables as parables of Jesus, for that is what I believe them to be. But it does not thereby necessarily follow that the picture of the designer that emerges from the pattern is in all respects the picture of the historical Jesus. Even if it were completely accurate as far as the evidence of these parables is concerned, it would still be incomplete, for the Gospels contain, of course, much else besides these tales.

The profile that emerges is, nevertheless, a striking one. Here, first, is a storyteller who delighted in *scenes of human life*. The gaze is across the gamut of everyday peasant experience: in the fields; at a family feast; on the streets and squares where beggars lay and labourers hoped for work; on dangerous country roads. Here are the kings and landowners upon whose whim and wealth so much of the social order depended. Here too are their trusted bond-servants, private armies, trading partners and impecunious tenants. Here are the familiar figures of Jewish establishment and piety: priest, Levite and Pharisee. Here also are the characters on the edge of acceptability: toll-collecting collaborators; a youthful runaway; a hated Samaritan. Without exception the human beings are meant to be real humans – not necessarily actual individuals, but real in the sense that they are not idealized demigods or demonized hate figures. And though there are plenty of signs that the stories are meant to carry significance far beyond the particular situation they depict, there is no sign that they

invite us to take our gaze off the human world and pass
quickly to some unseen or divine reality 'beyond'.

In Jewish thought that divine reality was absolutely
fundamental – the given framework in which everything
was viewed. The storyteller was not denying it; but neither
did he need to argue for it or assert it. His crucial burden
seemed to be that a new outlook *on the world* was called for
both by ancient faith and by current crisis.

However, the stories seem to have been more than invitations just to *view* the world differently. They imply that
specific action is called for. They are far removed from
being pleasant homespun tales about the virtues of neighbourliness or thrift. They picture a way of costly peace in
a time of national tension. They offer enemies and oppressors as examples of surprising compassion, frustrated
fellow countryfolk as examples of dangerous rebellion.
They hauntingly propose the welcome of outcasts to real
banquets. Sometimes the action called for is simply to
wait: it does no good to try and root out the weeds from
your field, or the enemies from your land, when the time is
not ripe.

This action is seen as *a way of wisdom*. There is an inner
logic in all the stories, so earthy that it has often been
missed. People do things that are seen, often in a surprising
or even humorous way, to make sense. You have an uneaten
spread on the table? Well, wouldn't it make sense to invite
the hungry? You know that your pagan overlords are cruel
and grasping? Well, can't you see the folly of not playing
their game? This wisdom is often embodied in narrative
movement, which is why the 'spiritual' interpretations often
seem so wooden, static and inappropriate. The shrewd
manager's master and the worldly judge, for instance,
change during the course of their stories.

The particular thrust of the stories in their social context
is to *subvert nationalism*. There were various kinds of

'nationalism' about, as we have seen: the accommodating policy of the Sadducees and Temple establishment; the strict piety of the Pharisees; the revolutionary aspirations of the Zealots. But the storyteller, it seems, saw his people as a whole as being on a collision course with their Roman rulers. In quite startling ways he seems to counsel collusion rather than collision. Trade with their dirty money; go to their bawdy wedding feasts. Lay on a welcoming party for a rebel son who has 'slept' with Gentile prostitutes and fed Gentile pigs; imagine the possibility that a customs collector might have his prayer answered. Recognize the true piety and generosity that exists among 'them' as well as among 'you'.

In this context the stories offer pictures of both *reversal and reconciliation*. Those familiar with the stories have got used to the reversals and need a new effort of imagination to recover the original shock: that a beggar should be found safe in the bosom of Abraham while the successful rich man burns in torment; that a Samaritan should act as neighbour while a priest and a Levite pass by. The younger son who has squandered the family inheritance in a degraded life-style is welcomed back with a great celebration while the upright (and uptight) older brother stands aloof and oddly estranged. But the storyteller's strain is not that of the simplistic revolutionary who merely wants to turn existing power structures on their head. He wants the rich men to learn to reach out to the poor at their gates and so stay on the same side of the yawning gulf as them after death. The Samaritan is not shown to the lawyer as a figure to make him feel condemned but as an example to follow. The father wants *both* sons at the party. The subversion and surprise permeate the stories in such a lively way that it is quite wrong to see the teller as 'for' or 'against' any social grouping as such. A wealthy landowner is as likely to be the hero as a poor widow.

Finally, the stories are filled with both *warning and hope*. In this sense they are the tales of a prophet in true Old Testament style. Although the warnings are couched in tales of earthy wisdom, as we have seen, wisdom for the Jewish people was not merely a secular matter. It was rooted in the order of a creator God. And the warnings of judgement and disaster waiting around the corner for those who failed to heed the way of wisdom would have been understood quite instinctively by both speaker and hearers as prophecies of God's action. This was not a remote and distant God, but one seen as intimately involved in the machinations of rulers and the affairs of their subjects. Tragically, as in the Old Testament, this was to be action *against* the very people through whom God had chosen to work out his will in the world. But it goes against the whole spirit of topsy-turvy reversal in the parables to see that action as final. Rather, it was to be the painful means whereby narrow nationalism was overthrown and God's 'people' no longer confined to a single race.

But there is also the golden thread of hope. These are not simply 'stories with a moral', giving guidance about human behaviour. They open up new windows of possibility. They point to the presence of God at work in the world in forgotten and unsuspected places: in a seed falling in good soil, finding its way despite the many barren spots it could have landed; in a judge administering justice, despite professed unbelief and carelessness; in a landowner providing for the needs of day labourers, even though they have only worked an hour. 'The kingdom of God is like this': not in the sense that an unseen, spiritual order of things may somehow be compared to this mundane scene, but in the sense that *in* such mundane scenes, God rules. 'Like this' – 'in this' – but, by implication, *not* like that, in that: not in the political savvy of the Sadducees, or the Pharisees' protective and divisive brand of holiness, or the Zealots' call to arms. Not, indeed, in any vision of merely national identity and freedom. Amid all the sombre warnings runs the joyful note. Look and see. God's rule is *here*.

Bibliography

Bailey, Kenneth E., *Poet and Peasant* and *Through Peasant Eyes: A Literary–Cultural Approach to the Parables in Luke*. Grand Rapids, Michigan: Eerdmans, 1976, 1980, combined edition 1983.
A rich source of fascinating insights from one immersed in the culture of the Near East.

Blomberg, Craig L., *Interpreting the Parables*. Leicester: Apollos, 1990.
A useful introduction with comprehensive coverage both of the parables themselves and of questions concerning methods of approach to them. Understands parables as each containing a certain number of 'points'.

Borsch, Frederick Houk, *Many Things in Parables: Extravagant Stories of New Community*. Philadelphia: Fortress Press, 1988.
A brief but pithy treatment of the parables, with suggestive social applications.

Dodd, Charles H., *The Parables of the Kingdom*. Welwyn, England: James Nisbet, revised edition 1961, first published 1935.
The classic English treatment of the twentieth century, very influential despite its comparative brevity, popularizing the 'one-point' approach to interpretation.

Donahue, John R., *The Gospel in Parable: Metaphor, Narrative and Theology in the Synoptic Gospels*. Philadelphia: Fortress Press, 1988.
A good exploration of the significance of the parables in their Gospel contexts.

Drury, John, *The Parables in the Gospels: History and Allegory*. London: SPCK, 1985.
A very useful study of the parables in relation both to their Old Testament background and to their Gospel contexts. Sceptical about the possibility of returning to the words or intention of Jesus.

Etchells, Ruth, *A Reading of the Parables of Jesus*. London: Darton, Longman & Todd, 1998.
Important and intriguing insights from a thoroughgoing literary perspective, and demonstrating the importance of that perspective for theology.

Hedrick, Charles W., *Parables as Poetic Fictions: The Creative Voice of Jesus*. Peabody, Massachusetts: Hendrickson, 1994.
Seeks to demonstrate that we should not look for any 'meaning' in the parables beyond the surface.

Herzog II, William R., *Parables as Subversive Speech: Jesus as Pedagogue of the Oppressed*. Louisville, Kentucky: Westminster John Knox Press, 1994.
Analyses a selection of parables using a sociological framework, and sheds much light on some difficult texts.

Hultgren, Arland J., *The Parables of Jesus: A Commentary*. Grand Rapids, Michigan: Eerdmans, 2000.
The latest comprehensive overview.

Jeremias, Joachim, *The Parables of Jesus*, S. H. Hooke (tr.). London: SCM, revised edition 1963.
The most influential work on the parables in the last century. Sought to locate the parables in their setting in the ministry of Jesus, and trace their developing forms as they were handed down in the early church, to the point where they were incorporated in the Gospels. Much useful historical material, even if many conclusions could now be challenged from different angles.

——, *Rediscovering the Parables*. London: SCM, 1966.
Abridged edition of the work cited above, omitting some technical material.

Longenecker, Richard N. (ed.), *The Challenge of Jesus' Parables*. Grand Rapids, Michigan: Eerdmans, 2000.
Summarizes some scholarly opinions and suggests something of the contemporary relevance of the stories.

Scott, Bernard Brandon, *Hear Then the Parable: A Commentary on the Parables of Jesus*. Minneapolis: Fortress Press, 1989.
A lengthy, comprehensive treatment, drawing together insights from historical, social and literary studies. Not an easy read, but useful for reference, and repays study.

Shillington, V. George (ed.), *Jesus and His Parables: Interpreting the Parables of Jesus Today*. Edinburgh: T&T Clark, 1997.
A useful collection of essays exploring the social context of the parables in accessible fashion. Good as a supplement to Bailey; an easier read but less detail.

Stegemann, Ekkehard W. and Wolfgang. *The Jesus Movement: A Social History of Its First Century*, O. C. Dean, Jr (tr.). Edinburgh: T&T Clark, 1999.
A detailed work of reference.

Westermann, Claus, *The Parables of Jesus in the Light of the Old Testament*. Edinburgh: T&T Clark, 1990.
An interesting introductory account of how the speech forms of the Old Testament relate to the parables, in the light of recent general studies in linguistics.

Wright, N. Tom, *The New Testament and the People of God*. London: SPCK, 1992.
A detailed account of the background of the New Testament in first-century Judaism.

——, *Jesus and the Victory of God*. London: SPCK, 1996.
An in-depth consideration of the aims of Jesus.

Wright, Stephen I., *The Voice of Jesus: Studies in the Interpretation of Six Gospel Parables*. Carlisle: Paternoster, 2000.
Reconsiders the history of parable interpretation with reference to six parables peculiar to Luke, and offers proposals for a contemporary basis for interpretation. Includes accounts of some interesting earlier parable interpretations.